AF604349

DOGNITIVE THERAPY

Laura Vissaritis is a qualified dog behaviourist with many years of experience. She formulated the 'Dognitive Therapy' approach to dog training, helping thousands of people not only develop better relationships with their dogs but also improve their own lives. Laura lives in Victoria with her Staffordshire bull terrier, Chester, and rescue dog, Alma.

Laura Vissaritis

DOGNITIVE THERAPY

TO CHANGE YOUR DOG'S BEHAVIOUR, FIRST YOU MUST CHANGE YOUR OWN

MICHAEL JOSEPH
an imprint of
PENGUIN BOOKS

MICHAEL JOSEPH

UK | USA | Canada | Ireland | Australia
India | New Zealand | South Africa | China

Penguin Books is part of the Penguin Random House group of companies
whose addresses can be found at global.penguinrandomhouse.com.

First published by Penguin Random House Australia Pty Ltd, 2017

1 3 5 7 9 10 8 6 4 2

Text copyright © Laura Vissaritis, 2017

The moral right of the author has been asserted.

All rights reserved. Without limiting the rights under copyright reserved above, no part of this publication may be reproduced, stored in or introduced into a retrieval system, or transmitted, in any form or by any means (electronic, mechanical, photocopying, recording or otherwise), without the prior written permission of both the copyright owner and the above publisher of this book.

Cover design by Louisa Maggio © Penguin Random House Australia Pty Ltd
Text design by Samantha Jayaweera © Penguin Random House Australia Pty Ltd
Cover photograph by Alex Cearns/Houndstooth Studio
Illustrations by Louisa Maggio © Penguin Random House Australia Pty Ltd
Typeset in Adobe Caslon by Samantha Jayaweera, Penguin Random House Australia Pty Ltd
Colour separation by Splitting Image Colour Studio, Clayton, Victoria
Printed and bound in Australia by Griffin Press, an accredited ISO AS/NZS
14001 Environmental Management Systems printer.

National Library of Australia
Cataloguing-in-Publication data:

Vissaritis, Laura, author
Dognitive therapy / Laura Vissaritis
9780143783497 (paperback)

Dogs – Training – Australia.
Dogs – Behaviour.
Dogs – Psychology.

penguin.com.au

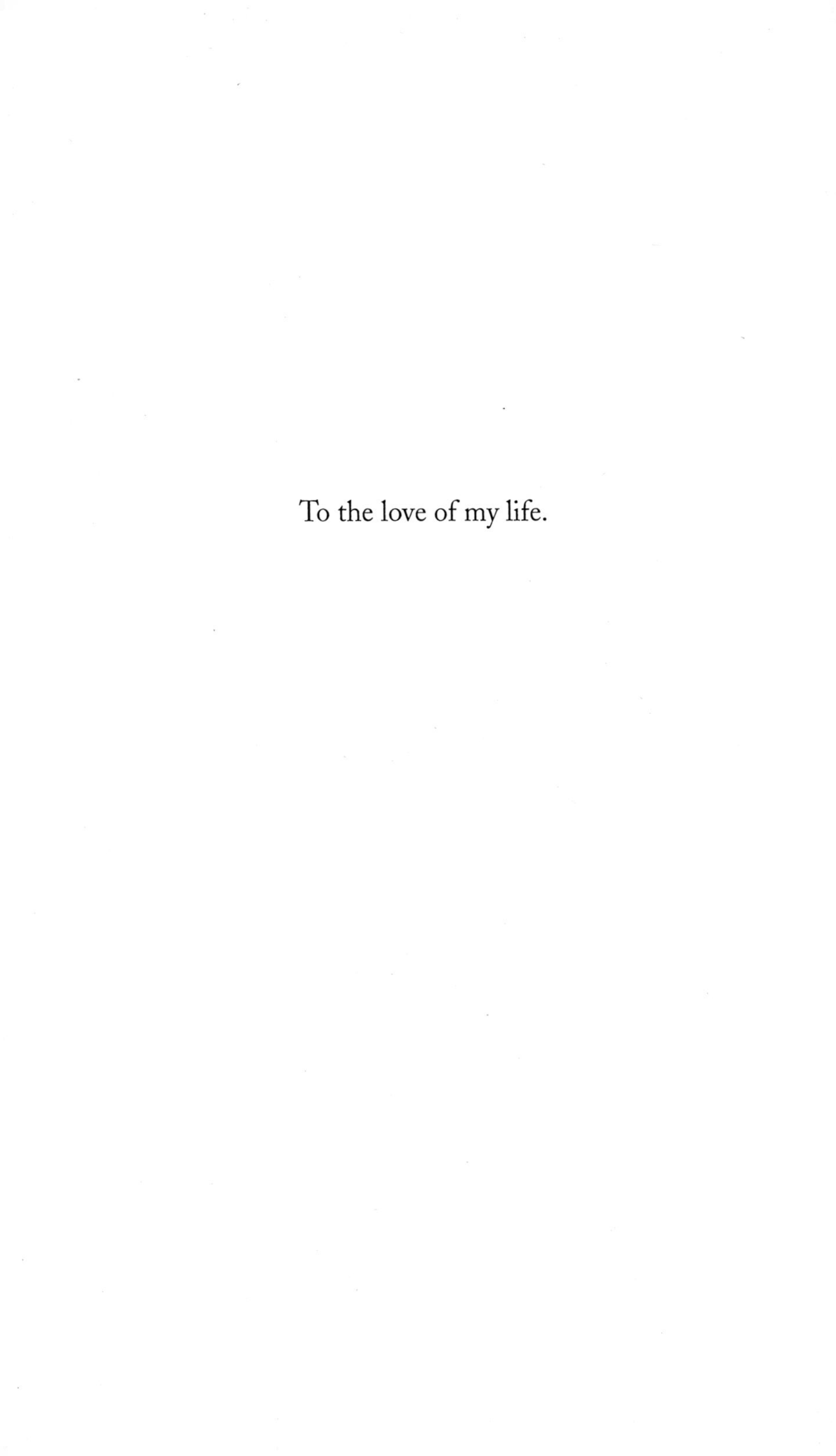

To the love of my life.

CONTENTS

Introduction

The cornerstone of my approach to dog training is that *dog training is not about dogs: it's about people.* Our dogs are a reflection of us. Every day, we make simple but critical mistakes that not only have consequences on our dogs' well-being but on our wellbeing too.

When it comes to self-improvement however, dogs can be our best teachers. They can challenge and motivate us to be our best. The purpose of this book is to show you how to be a happier and healthier person, all through understanding the world from your dog's perspective.

My first experience training dogs came when I was just a toddler. My mother always encouraged my gentle soul and determined mind, which were two things dogs seemed to love about me. I was lucky to have been taught the importance of respect and kindness at a young age, but within me there has always been an instinct for understanding animals.

In some ways then I have been training animals for thirty years. But the thing about learning is that it is never one directional. I have learnt just as much, if not more, from the dogs I have taught than they have from me. This is a lifelong journey, and while we can never know everything, we can continue to explore and discover. This is when we are at our best.

My education in animal behaviour was certainly thorough and holistic. I was taught every approach to dog training, including the uses of prong and e-collars. The place I originally trained at included practical lessons, where kennel dogs and compulsory correction collars were a part of our program. In complete ignorance, I took control of dogs and experimented my new techniques on them like guinea pigs.

I had initially embarked on my career as a dog behaviourist thinking that correcting a dog by inconsistently yanking the chain around their neck would stop them from misbehaving. And sometimes it did. But where was the trust? Where was the respect? It certainly wasn't coming from me, nor was it coming from the other end of my leash.

Many may shake their heads at me, and say, 'Laura, there is a science to positive punishment and correction. You don't understand the principles of learning.' (Adding something unpleasant to stop a dog's behaviour is called 'positive punishment', removing something your dog wants to stop a behaviour is called 'negative punishment'.)

I do understand the principles of learning. And I agree, there is a science to it. But there is also a science to building positive relationships, understanding motivations and setting dogs up for success not failure. I talk more about punishment later in the book, because I think it is important for every dog owner to understand the basic science behind it. I do use punishment techniques, as do all dog owners, including 'positive trainers'. Withholding food, walking away, ignoring your dog; these are all negative punishments. We are removing something our dog wants to stop an unwanted behaviour. Whilst these measures to change behaviour may be useful, dog training should be about empowering dogs to think positively. It should be about building relationships based on mutual trust and respect.

I am a permanent student with an insatiable hunger for learning. I am fascinated by research, always reading and studying, often expressing my enthusiasm for animal and human psychology to those who perhaps are a little less excited by it. Learning is one of my great loves and I am passionate about this subject.

I have studied at tertiary levels since I was seventeen. A Bachelor of Animal Science first gave me a taste for understanding non-human life. It introduced me to science, taught me to think in different ways, open my mind to possibilities and most importantly, to ask questions. A couple of years later, I found myself gravitating to a slightly different branch of science; a science that looked at human life forms, but in a very different way. Archaeology delved deep into the sediment of history, where I learnt more about our own species than I had initially intended to. Human evolution fascinates me: as a species we have changed in extraordinary ways, but this change has taken extraordinary time.

But change does take time. It is something I always remind my clients when taking their first step into the world of dog behaviour change. It is an emotional evolution if you like.

After graduating I returned to post-graduate study in Education. It was here that I discovered how to marry everything I knew about the natural world with teaching. After tireless persistence and some overbearing enthusiasm, I got my first real job. I became the youngest Wildlife Educator at

Zoos Victoria. It was a place I fell desperately in love with, where my zoo colleagues and I shared an insatiable passion for wildlife. Together, we met hundreds of thousands of children, many of whom now work in similar fields fighting for those without a voice and inspiring the next generation, just as we did.

Then one day, I met Chester. I found out about him through a Staffordshire bull terrier club and went to visit him, his parents and the humans that were responsible for his beginnings. He was a tiny, vulnerable ball on legs. He reminded me of a child in many ways; no prejudice or judgement, just an enthusiastic being with an open heart and mind, willing to meet another with the most optimistic expectations. The indiscriminate welcome he gave me as I sat down on the floor won my heart and I knew I could not leave him behind. I propped him up on the front seat of my unprepared car and just like that, his entire life came to depend on me.

Chester was just like all the animals I worked with at the zoo, except he was *my* responsibility. My love for him motivated me to learn more about dog behaviour. I watched him develop from an eight-week-old puppy into a strong and discerning adult. But no matter how old he gets, Chester will depend on me his entire life. It was clear that dog ownership was a lifelong responsibility.

Years went by as I combined my two great loves: being at the zoo and becoming a dog behaviourist. But along the way I realised I was missing something. The only way to make life better for dogs was to help the animals with the power to make real change: people. The next day, I began post-graduate research in Psychology. And as I continue further in my studies, I can see that there is an ironic simplicity to improving the life of a dog, because the art of *human* behaviour change is something 'experts' are still yet to master.

The human mind is a black box. It is the one part of the body that we still know relatively little about. It's a complex, multilayered mystery that is part of all of us, and the more we uncover revelations of the mind and our thoughts, the more we realise how much we still don't know. And that's what I love about it.

Dognitive therapy is a combination of my lifelong learning and the principles of cognitive behavioural therapy (CBT). CBT teaches us behavioural management strategies to cope with distress. When we implement these strategies, we can better handle our response to the environment we live in, making our lives more manageable no matter what we encounter in our day. During my interactions with dog owners, I encourage them to talk about their feelings, their frustrations and anxieties. I also ask them to consider the world from their dog's point of view. Dogs experience very similar emotions to us, including frustration and anxiety, but we tend to only notice it when they do something we don't like, such as digging up the backyard or growling at the dog next door.

You might not know it yet, but your dog is in many ways a reflection of you. And while you may not like to listen, and you may not want to see, your dog can tell you the honest truth about yourself.

So who are you? I don't expect you to answer that question just yet, because even I don't know how to answer that question about myself. If I asked my dog who I am – and if he could respond – he would say that I am quite highly-strung, often unsettled and not especially social. But at the same time, he would tell me that I am able to take the lead in times of uncertainty and that I am trustworthy and respectful.

If you think from your dog's perspective, you can probably give an accurate description of the person your dog sees. In fact, our dogs *can* tell us this, because who we are is communicated in their behaviour. Everything they do tells us a little bit about ourselves. We may not like the answers our dogs give us, but there is something elating about being able to recognise who you really are, who you could be and who you will be.

Chester is now seven years old. He is a deep thinker; a little needy and anxious if he doesn't feel in control. He is a sensitive, old soul and prefers my company to most others'. Hmm, that sounds a lot like me. I bet if you consider the character traits of your own dog, you'll find more than a few similarities with your own personality too.

Alma is my other canine love. She is much older than Chester, having been rescued from a puppy farm after no longer being able to breed. Along with her heavy baggage, she brought with her a long list of ailments. Alma no longer has ears, is partially paralysed from copious amounts of life-saving surgery, and suffers from arthritis. Her canines are completely worn down after gnawing and grinding her way through wired confines. Her little black belly sags to her knees as a reminder of the dutiful mothering she provided to many and her eyes tell the story of a long past of suffering. She is always tired. But that's okay. She is safe now.

When I first met Alma, she was very reactive, lunging at dogs in an attempt to control them with her teeth. Her tail was permanently positioned between her legs and she consistently displayed caution and distrust. I never trained Alma on a lead. And whilst she may be deaf, I have never stopped talking to her. Together we learnt to respect and trust each other and, three years later, Alma is quite a different dog. Her attitude towards life has been renewed. In her behaviour, I see trust and respect. I always see moments of contentedness, and even glimmers of complete happiness. In her, I see a reflection of the life she now has. The life she always deserved.

Although dogs are considered man's best friend, they are not considered equals in our society. People can purchase them, surrender them, and treat them as they see fit. People often treat dogs like objects. But they are sentient animals and we need to understand that our respect for them reflects the level of respect we have for ourselves.

Respecting others, particularly those who don't have a voice, shows great strength of character, because those without a voice can never say thank you. Helping those who can never thank us is the mark of a good person.

I know I can't make life better for every dog, but I can for yours. But only through helping you and changing the way you see this world and how you manage yourself within it. When a person sees their dog not just as a pet, but as a teacher and as a friend, then I have done my job. I know that both dog and owner will live happier and healthier lives.

This book is my gift to you, to help you grow, love and understand yourself through understanding the best 'person' you know: your dog.

Let's get started.

Did you know . . . *a dog's mind bears similarities to a 2½-year-old human child's? Research shows that dogs are highly intelligent, can understand up to 250 words and can even count.*

1.

Dognitive Therapy

The mind is arguably the most fascinating part of our bodies. It is the centre of control, the mediator between the conscious and subconscious and, ultimately, what makes us who we are.

Dognitive therapy for people and their dogs is my simplified version of cognitive behavioural therapy (CBT). CBT was originally designed as a treatment for depression and has become an empirically supported psychological treatment for a range of human disorders including anxiety, addiction, compulsion and even chronic pain. It is based around analysing how our thinking patterns affect our emotions and behaviours. The theory behind it posits an interplay between three core aspects of the mind: one's cognition (beliefs, self-perception and general thoughts), one's affective state (their feelings, temperament and emotions) and one's behaviours.

During CBT a person is encouraged to challenge unhelpful thinking patterns and look for more rational ways to approach situations. It can help people understand that their irrational fears are not 'real' and that the world won't end when they face them.

CBT is now a widespread and multifaceted practice with a range of branches reaching out from its central ideas. One of these is acceptance and commitment therapy, or ACT, although ACT psychologists may claim it is an approach in its own right. This therapy contains elements of traditional CBT as well as useful aspects of mindfulness, and is often recommended for children experiencing behavioural disorders including anxiety and aggression. Naturally, as a dog behaviourist, I have considered how these human treatments can be applied to behaviour modification in dogs, particularly methods most effective for young children. With young children and dogs bearing many cognitive similarities, the psychological approaches are in many ways connected.

ACT encourages you to exist in the present among the unhelpful thinking and to mentally move towards more positive thinking. It invites you to open up to unpleasant thoughts and feelings in the moment, and to live with them, accepting that they are just thoughts, nothing more, nothing less. The idea is that when we sit with our inner anxieties and fears, accepting that they are just thoughts, then we can find a better understanding of what is actually true and real, moving towards more valued behaviours. ACT can be broken down into these three steps:

- Accept your reactions and be present
- Choose a valued direction
- Take action

Of course, imparting this knowledge to your dogs is a little tricky. You can't just tell your dog to be in the moment, accept unpleasant feelings and choose a more positive thought process based on their values. But there are ways to apply ACT to help improve your dog's thinking habits.

Example

If a dog feels fearful, phobic or anxious, they can undergo an exposure therapy called desensitisation. Ensuring the dog is never pushed past their threshold, we can allow them to safely observe the stimulus that alarms them at a comfortable distance, feel the uncertainty just a little, sit with it and overcome it. It is honestly magical to see a dog stand in the face of their fear, look it in the eye and accept it. One of my favourite parts of dog behaviour modification is safely exposing a dog to a stimulus they are unsure of and watching their gorgeous mind think, analyse and decide on what to do all on their own. It is so important to empower that sense of control in your dog.

When you do it properly, your dog will watch that other dog in the distance, or the man across the road in the hoodie, or that skateboarder in the alley and will think, make a decision, and then look back at you. That moment is one of those times in which you pop the proverbial champagne and celebrate with your dog. You have empowered them to control their impulses, to think for themselves and to make a safe decision. You have given them strength and improved their life, all the while letting them think they did it all on their own.

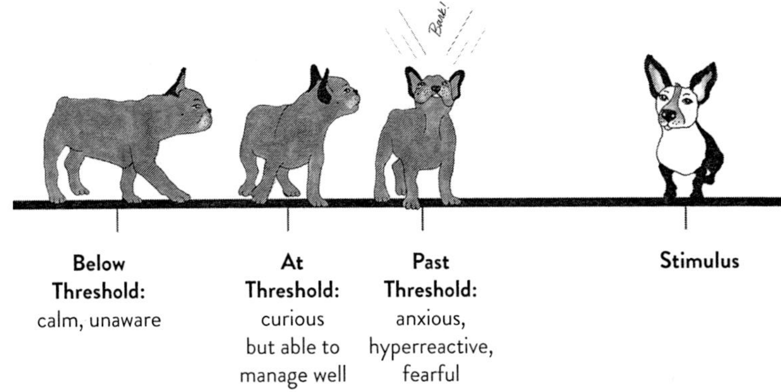

I am privileged to work alongside incredible people in this field who have dedicated their lives to researching canine and human psychology. These are people I look to and learn from, so that I can tell you all about what we find. I don't claim to have all the answers, but what I do have is emotional intelligence. I am a person who understands people's motivations. I can relate to people and appreciate where they are coming from. I read, look at the evidence, question it and find ways to best approach difficult situations. I am a sceptic, but I am also an optimist. My passion for making life better for dogs and their owners is unquenchable, and what I see in this world are millions of people with their pets in desperate need of help. Not just because of poor behaviour, but because they exist together in relationships without ever being open to experiencing the magic of them.

Everybody's life can be better. Everybody deserves the chance to experience genuine happiness. But life is not a journey toward finding happiness. Instead, happiness exists in moments throughout the journey. It exists in moments of magic in which our partner makes us laugh, when that sun settles on to the back of our shoulders or when our dog looks to us with complete trust and respect. These are the moments to live for and they are right in front of you, right now. What moments really matter to you?

Dogs already know this. They are excellent patients for CBT and ACT. They are willing to learn new patterns of thinking, and are accepting of the moments in life that present them with unease. But, they are also vulnerable like we are, inevitably taking more steps backwards before they can move ahead without looking back.

Research shows that under CBT and ACT, at least 50 per cent of depressed patients will relapse. Seventy to 80 per cent of patients experiencing more than one type of disorder in combination with depression will also relapse. In dog training, this will also happen. You will have moments in which you are completely elated by your dog's training progression. You will feel a sense of accomplishment when you notice that you and your dog are calmer, more cooperative and more controlled in situations that previously resulted in chaos. But you will invariably experience days of cold, hard failure. Remember, this is all part of the journey. What's important is to persevere. Celebrate the tiny, miniscule highs. The more you collect, the bigger they get.

HOW TO APPLY DOGNITIVE THERAPY TO YOUR LIFE

We can't change for the better until we recognise the problem with ourselves and, almost invariably, the problem is our thoughts. We tend to mull over molehills to the point where they seem like insurmountable mountains, and we become exhausted before we even attempt to climb them.

Have you ever thought to yourself:

- I can't do it
- It's too hard
- I don't have time
- It's not working
- It will never work
- I give up

These are the unhelpful thoughts that creep into our minds whenever we are faced with a challenge that takes time and effort, and where results are not immediately tangible. The thing about these thoughts is that they are true, if you believe them. Choose not to believe them, and they become false. Your mind ultimately holds the power to your reality, and so unhelpful thinking patterns will faithfully stick by your side if you keep feeding them. Ultimately, how you think, is up to you.

The mindfulness strategies in this book are an excellent start to improving our approach to thinking, remembering that every thought we have affects our behaviour and that each behaviour we have affects our dogs. Sitting with our thoughts and analysing them helps us to understand them, judge them and make decisions that are rational.

If we can persuade dogs to sit with their thoughts in times of stress, we can encourage thinking strategies that help them decide what is threatening, what is benign and what is positive. If we set our dogs up for success, we can usually create environments that elicit positive emotions and empower them to make logical choices. CBT, or should I say, DT (dognitive therapy), contains principles that ultimately empower self-belief. When our dogs are confident in their thoughts, they make choices that are conducive to a healthy and happy life.

SUMMARY

Unhelpful thinking patterns affect not just your behaviour, but your dog's behaviour too. Start to implement CBT and ACT into your every day life and lead by example. Set your dog up for success in times of uncertainty. Encourage them to safely observe, sit with some hesitation and make a positive choice to accept and move on.

Try this in your every day life too. Stress is inevitable, but you always have the choice of how to respond to it.

2.

The Beginning of Leadership

My definition of leadership is: 'To empower others to walk alongside you because they want to, not because they have to.' This is what we should aim for with our dogs.

So, where do we start? The first step is to identify the bones of leadership; the basic building blocks of a relationship based on mutual trust and respect.

There are two common threads throughout this book that are essentially the holy grail to dognitive therapy.

The first one is called CPR, the attributes of a true leader:

- Consistent
- Patient
- Respectful

The second is called the 3 Cs. These are the behaviours and emotions we want to reinforce and instil in those we lead. We briefly touch on these in this chapter, but we will go into more depth later on.

- Calm
- Cooperative
- Controlled

WHO COMES TO MIND WHEN YOU THINK OF A GREAT LEADER?

Who you see as a leader is based on your values. For me, names like Pam Ahern, Lyn White, the Dalai Lama and Martin Luther King spring to mind amongst many others. All of these people define leadership to me because they have endured great struggles, been a part of revolutionary change and despite being kicked down, they all got up and kept going. They have provided inspiring words, believed in their passions and strived for the best in not just themselves but also in others. All very different in their leadership styles, but all inherent leaders in their own right.

Those who embody leadership may be different for you. Who we see as leaders are those who we connect with, and while there may be hundreds of different people who come to our minds, one thing we can all agree on is that they inspire greatness.

You may not know it yet, but you too are a leader, and you are about to inspire greatness in the one being who needs you more than anyone else. This book is a guide to improving your mindset so that it can be reflected in the outlook and behaviours of your dog.

Whilst dogs may indeed be man's best friend, there is one major difference between us and them. This difference is one that often causes conflict between the two species and one reason why so many dogs end up in shelters. Humans have the luxury of growing up, gaining independence and becoming leaders one day. Dogs don't. They are essentially eternal toddlers. And whilst they inevitably grow into adulthood, they can never truly live an independent life. Understandably, frustrations fly from both parties, resulting in tension, anger and behavioural problems. A dog truly is for life, each and every day.

One thing to realise is that we are here not as a dog's 'owner' but as their leader. Dogs are not our right, they are our privilege and it is our duty to provide a lifelong relationship of trust. Our ability to provide this to those at our mercy says a lot more about us than you may realise, and it all starts with three simple words: consistency, patience, respect.

THE PRINCIPLES OF LEARNING AND REINFORCEMENT

Although behaviour is influenced by multiple factors, including genetic predisposition, life experiences and the environment, most of our behaviours have been learnt. Think about everything you know, think and do and you will agree that at some point in your life you have learnt it through experience. It might have been taught to you, you might have figured it out yourself, or there might have been a life event that left you learning something new and important. The reason why we are all here today, functioning as we are, is because our behaviours have been reinforced.

For a behaviour to be reinforced, it needs to be rewarded so that it occurs again. When a behaviour is rewarded, it creates a connection between the action and the consequence, and a prediction that when that behaviour occurs again, it will be rewarded. This type of learning is called operant conditioning. I can think of countless behaviours that have been reinforced in our lives and these principles of reinforcement for our dogs are exactly the same.

Behaviour + timely reward = behaviour occurs again

Just as behaviours that are helpful in life are reinforced, behaviours that are unhelpful and sometimes dysfunctional in our lives are also reinforced. Examples that come to mind are anxious and avoidant behaviours. Although anxiety is essential for survival, many people suffer from an anxiety disorder. People predisposed to the disorder are more likely to learn unhelpful thinking strategies in life, but these thoughts and behaviours need to have been reinforced for them to exist and continue throughout life.

An anxiety disorder is the most common underlying cause of unwanted dog behaviours. Life is full of unpredictable and uncontrollable challenges that are thrown our way each day. For dogs, it is no different, except they have even less control in this world than we do. Coming to terms with this allows us to apply empathy and respect, accepting that some of the behaviours we expect from our dogs are actually unrealistic and unfair.

Example

I never allow children to approach my dog Chester. I am the one he depends on to keep him safe and if I can't control his environment, then why should he trust me? Instead, I let Chester feel like he is in control of these situations. I ask the child to sit on the floor and if Chester chooses to go and say hello, they can pat him. If he chooses not to, then that is okay. In fact, that is a learning opportunity for the child. They learn that Chester is not an object and that we should respect others' choices.

If I didn't provide leadership to Chester, and allowed any child to approach him, I could risk the safety of Chester as well as the child. Chester might learn that growling makes the child go away, reinforcing this behaviour and making him more likely to growl again.

I want to reinforce Chester's experience with children, making it a positive one. I have done this by allowing him to make choices, never feeling threatened, and if he does approach a child for a pat, there is a good chance he will get a treat. This is how you reinforce what you want, keeping in mind that it is just as easy, if not easier, to inadvertently reinforce behaviours you don't want. It is something you need to be on top of when training and CPR is instrumental in the success of rewarding the right behaviours.

As you read through this book, keep in mind the fundamentals of building a healthy relationship with others: consistency, patience and respect.

Apply the 3-2-1 approach whenever an opportunity presents itself each day. Find opportunities to be consistent and patient with others, and take the time just to look after yourself.

Lastly, start to think about the positive behaviours we look for in others. The ones that we want to acknowledge and reinforce, particularly with our dogs and children. Remember the 3 Cs: calm, cooperative and controlled.

We will come back to all of these ideas throughout this book. Understanding and implementing them into your life, your training and your relationships will leave you and your dog happier, healthier and closer than ever before.

Did you know . . . *the canid was the earliest group of animals still extant that belongs to the order 'carnivora'? Their history spans some forty million years, where their cooperative adaptations led to a genera whose predatory capacity dominated much of the old world.*

3.
CPR

The three traits of being consistent, patient and respectful are difficult to master! Time and effort are required, which are two things humans tend to instinctively avoid. For me, this poses a regular challenge with clients, and it is usually the cause of all their problems in the first place. One story that comes to mind is the story of Jake and the Duncans.

CASE STUDY

Jake was a black Lab. Only ten months of age and full of life, he was the quintessential tween, with every manipulative trick up his sleeve. He barked when he wanted to come inside, he obsessively pawed at his owners' laps when he wanted attention, he jumped on the table and kitchen bench when he wanted whatever was on top of it and he even sent peemails in his owners' shoes, particularly Barry's, the husband and father of the house. Jake was skating on thin ice, the kind of ice that is between a loving home and the confines of a pound.

I met the Duncans after they had paid three other dog

trainers who claimed Jake was 'a little different'. Trainers told the family that he probably couldn't be helped and that they would be better to find him another home. One trainer even suggested Jake be put to sleep! I was welcomed into their lovely home and within one second of my arrival, Jake jumped on me, barked, urinated on my leg, then ran off. 'Well hello to you too, Jake,' I said as the family's mouths dropped in humiliation and shame at Jake's unfavourable antics. Julie chased Jake around the house and up the stairs, lunging at him, each time belly flopping to the floor with the lead but no dog. Jake finally tired and after another five minutes of chasing him around the kitchen table, Julie was able to wrangle him to the floor and wrap the lead around his neck. Once we had all caught our breath, we sat down to talk about this lanky canine whose fate was questionable.

Sometimes I go to a consultation and it feels like it is in slow motion. I watch the dog and then the owner and find myself fascinated by how owners interact with their dogs. With Jake and the Duncans, it was no different. Julie quickly forgot Jake was on-lead and he began to herd the table, walking around it, pushing into everyone's laps as they unconsciously put their hand on his back and began scratching it. He then barked at Julie, to which she responded with a 'Jake, no' and Jake moved on to me. Jake barked, nudged, pawed, slobbered, then barked again, before moving away and lifting his leg on the corner wall closest to me. 'JAKE NO!' squealed Barry and Julie, and Jake found the scruff of his neck in the clutch of Barry's hand as he swiftly slid along the timber floor and into the backyard.

Jake was out of control. In fact, everyone there was out of control. There was no purpose for Jake, no direction, no guidance. Jake simply did not know what to do with himself, so he did whatever he wanted, all the time.

I let Jake back inside, found a treat in my bag and held it calmly at the table. Jake quickly responded and as I shoved it in his mouth, I picked up the lead. I took Jake over to the lounge room where there was more space and I let him do his worst. Jake knew I had another treat in my hand, so he nuzzled his nose in my hand to try and dig it out, then he jumped, barked, even howled, before attempting his grand finale of the jump whilst clawing into me and barking in my face. I stood there in absolute peace as his owners watched in horror. Within a few seconds, Jake let me go. He tried again, but for a shorter amount of time and then after five minutes of me standing like a lifeless mannequin, Jake stood down and sat.

At the exact moment, he got the treat that was in my hand.

I walked around the lounge with him on-lead and stopped. Jake sat and he got a treat. I walked again, stopped, Jake sat and he got two treats. We had embarked on a fun game where we were cooperating with each other and both getting what we wanted. I dropped the lead and walked off. Jake followed me and when I stopped, guess what he did? He sat. Guess what I did? I gave him three treats. We were playing CPR. I was consistently displaying my expectations. If at any time he tried his destructive repertoire, I *consistently* turned my back, ignored him, even walked away and closed the door momentarily. And yes, this is a form of punishment, known as negative punishment (removing a reward to stop an unwanted behaviour).

I was incredibly *patient*. I could see the frustration in Jake's owners' eyes when they told me about his problems and I made it clear that at any time they were feeling impatient, they must stop the training and have some time out. Patience is so important because you are effectively rewiring a neural pathway, from one behaviour to another. Sometimes this takes time, folks. This simple trick took five minutes to achieve, but

I promised Julie and Barry that as soon as I left, Jake would return to his old ways.

I always tell my clients that their dog will most likely regress back to their old ways the day after a session because they default to what their long-term memory tells them works. So the Duncans assured me they would practise this consistent approach, teach Jake to station to his bed when he wanted something, give him his dinner in a treat dispenser instead of a food bowl and increase his mind and body exercise routine each day. I returned a week later.

After knocking on the door, I heard two barks that I assumed were Jake's, but that was it. Barry opened the door with Jake on-lead and Jake sat without being asked. Barry slipped a yummy treat to Jake and I walked inside. Barry allowed Jake to sniff me politely before receiving calm praise and I followed the two proud blokes into the lounge. Jake was escorted to his bed where he had a chew toy and as Barry let the lead go, Jake began entertaining himself with his chew. Jake had just been for his morning run and as part of his consistent daily routine, he had time to contentedly rest on his bed for a couple hours.

It was so lovely to see. Jake had direction and routine. He knew what was expected of him and his owners understood that his behaviours were a reflection of their leadership. The Duncans had done me proud, but more so they had done Jake proud. There had been no reports of peemails since Barry began to engage with Jake more and Julie reported that Jake had not jumped up at her since we last met.

It's such a simple rule, CPR. Keeping things consistent and respectful, whilst being patient is an essential but easy tool to incorporate into your everyday life, with your everyday relationships. Jake is now a middle-aged fellow. I still receive emails (not peemails!) from Barry and Julie, showing off what

Jake is up to. How he won the obedience trial championship and how they couldn't imagine life without him.

WHAT IS YOUR DOG REALLY THINKING?

Is your dog happy? How do you know? Is their happiness demonstrated by a wagging tail or the excitable greeting upon your return? How do you know if this is happiness?

These questions got me thinking about our relationship with our best mates, wondering if they are happy or if we are just convincing ourselves that they are. Perhaps we are afraid to learn the truth. What if our dogs were telling us something completely different? What if the connection we thought we had was not mutual?

'Please let me be the person my dog thinks I am.' If you haven't read this quote before, it implies that dogs already think their owner is wonderful and that the owner should strive to become what their dog sees in them. I think dogs definitely see their owner as they truly are; only I don't believe dogs use the rose-coloured lens like in this quote. A dog may wag his tail at his owner and stand by her side even if she is the antithesis of wonderful. But, not because he trusts or respects her. Not because he thinks she is wonderful, but because he has no choice.

Dogs are our most intuitive friends and their behaviours are an honest reflection of who we are. Don't be afraid to find out. Our dogs' intentions are favourable and they want you to be your best. They benefit from this too. If they could write a description of their ideal leader, they would jot down something very simple. It would include the basic attributes of a good character, someone who is confident but calm and someone who knows how to give CPR: a *consistent*, *patient* and *respectful* approach. It would look a little like this:

Dog: My leader is consistent. Everything they say has meaning behind it and they follow through. Their fair expectations guide me to succeed, not fail, and as a result I feel confident in their leadership.

My leader understands that while I am devoted to them, I am not fluent in their language. Instead, I speak to them through my body language.

I am not their child and as much as they might like to direct their parenting needs on to my care, they acknowledge that I am a dog and I will never be able to fulfil their expectations as a human being.

I will follow their guidance as they consistently and patiently provide a path toward health and happiness for us together. They respect my feelings. They know I have emotions, that I think a lot and experience fear, happiness, anxiety, sadness, and even love.

I am not a robot. Sometimes, I don't want to meet that other dog, or lie down on the cold, wet grass, and my leader respects that. I know I have a fur coat, but I still yearn to be beside them indoors.

They know I will disobey them, sometimes I won't listen and I will disappoint them at times. They will disappoint me too, but that is a part of any honest and real relationship. We are together because we want to be and despite our failings, we still work on our relationship each and every day. We trust and respect each other completely.

Does this sound like you and your dog? To a dog, CPR is imperative to a positive relationship. Are you giving your dog CPR each day?

CONSISTENCY

The definition of consistency is 'acting in the same way in order to be fair'.

Being consistent provides structure in our lives and indeed helps to build trust and respect in our relationships. To have structure, we need to be able to foresee the immediate future and manage the present. So having a consistent routine that we stick to each day, helps us to feel in control of our lives.

If you asked your mind what the two things it needs to function optimally are, it would say, *control and predictability.*

Everything in our mind comes down to these two factors. Whether we can predict or control our environment determines how we feel and how we behave.

Example

Imagine your dog has been attacked by another dog on the corner of your street. Dogs are highly intelligent and emotional animals just like humans. This means that they also need to control and predict their environment. The day after the attack, when you and your dog step out for your daily walk, you head to the street corner where the incident happened. If you look at your dog, you may see their body language change. The hair on their back will stiffen (a reaction called piloerection), their ears may move forward and their body and tail might freeze. They may pull towards the corner anticipating the perpetrating dog will be there. Or, they may pull away and try to avoid the walk altogether. Whatever their behaviour, your dog is communicating their emotional state to you. Not only are they predicting the outcome of that threat, they are trying to control their environment at the same time.

As humans, we behave like this too. We need to predict and control our environment, or we start to show signs of anxiety and fear, just like dogs. We have one advantage over dogs however and that is that this world is designed for humans. The world makes so much more sense from our point of view. Because of this, we must always strive to provide a consistently predictable and controllable environment for our dogs. We will look at this more practically later, in Chapter 5.

There is no doubt that building positive relationships with others is important. But that doesn't mean it is easy. Inconsistent leadership is probably the biggest issue people have in their relationships and the most common examples are people's relationships with their dogs and children.

When an expectation is set, it must be followed through. If it can't be followed through, it shouldn't be expected.

Example

If you ask your child to put away a toy and they don't, most likely it's because they know there is no consequence either way. Why would your child waste energy and comply when there is nothing in it for them?

Have you ever been too tired or busy to follow through and just ended up putting the toys away yourself?

What does your child learn? They learn that you won't follow through and that you don't mean what you say.

As their leader and protector, do they respect you?

The same applies to your dog. Being inconsistent sets you up for a relationship without trust or respect. Many people have said to me that their dog won't listen to them. Trust me, they are definitely listening to you, but they are hearing a whole different conversation!

In every relationship, we look for honesty, trustworthiness and respect. A key to attaining these is to ensure that our words are consistent with our deeds.

Sometimes we make promises we can't live up to, and while our intentions may have been honourable at the time, when it comes time to follow through, many of us don't. Inconsistent behaviours can affect our relationships because those who we are making promises to stop believing us. This also changes how people perceive you. They begin seeing you as unreliable, untrustworthy and sometimes even as a person with an ulterior motive.

The same applies to our dogs. If we move one way, but finish up in the opposite direction, eventually our dogs stop following us. In other words, if we do not follow through with what we have set out to do, we appear unpredictable and therefore lose trust and respect from them shortly after.

There is an internal consistency that is important in all of us, not just for ourselves but for those we influence around us. In our work life, having clear values and attitudes attracts others to us. People know that you have confidence in your beliefs and that you can be trusted to work and live true to your ethics.

In your relationship with a life partner, an internally consistent alignment means you will always follow through with what you say; your promises are truths and your values and morals in that relationship are constant.

Additionally, a similar approach to parenting results in

favourable outcomes between you and your child. When you mean something you say and consistently follow through, your child is less likely to seek to manipulate situations, push boundaries or test weaknesses. Children soon learn that a consistent parent is one who can be trusted, who always means what they say and whose values are persistent.

Many life-coaching experts argue that being consistent actually hinders people's performance in relationships. They liken being consistent to being a bit of a know-it-all. But there is a difference between being consistent in what you believe is right and being a concrete-minded know-it-all. If we don't follow through with our beliefs then we can never expect anyone to believe that we mean what we say. Who could possibly trust or respect someone who doesn't mean what they say?

It's unavoidable that sometimes we will make mistakes and follow through on the wrong decision. For example, we might persist with a work disagreement or make our child do homework even though it's too hard for them, but part of this life journey is to acknowledge our mistakes, learn from them and make amends.

Every day I hear dog owners commanding their pets to behave in a way that is unrealistic or confusing, or in a way where they don't follow through. The 'sit, sit, sit, sit, sit . . .' command where the dog doesn't sit and walks off is ten seconds of life wasted. That dog doesn't respect that person, the person doesn't respect their command and, together, the relationship is not strengthened in anyway.

Yes, you will make mistakes with your dog – many times, in fact. You will ask your dog to sit a thousand times without them listening and you will disempower them by expecting something they don't understand – you will inevitably set them up to fail. But you will learn from this and together you will grow. Think about the world from your dog's point of view. Only ask something of them if you can be consistent and fair.

PATIENCE

Patience is defined as 'the capacity to accept delay without becoming annoyed or anxious'.

We live in an increasingly impatient world. Unsurprisingly as a result, people are becoming less happy. Synonymous with patience is tolerance and without tolerance, we cannot cooperate within our relationships, our community or our society.

Intolerant people are easily frustrated and redirect their emotions on to others around them. We see this in traffic jams and on social media. When intolerant people are protected behind a car door or computer screen, they are more likely to lash out at others. This provides a safety buffer for unregulated and abusive behaviours.

Arguably, the most dire situations of intolerance are within domestic settings. Couples who lose patience for each other often engage in arguments, heartache, divorce and even violence. Life seems to be getting busier. Expectations are higher than ever and pressures to be successful are widespread. People fall for the pressures dictated by modern society and the media, believing that success and happiness is based on what you have, not who you are. With this new reality being unachievable, how can anyone ever feel good about themselves? There is no room for patience and understanding within ourselves, so how could we possibly expect to have it for others?

I see lack of patience and frustration in dog owners every day. It is a major issue in dog training, because training requires effort and time. In addition to this, dogs do not speak our language and this makes it more difficult for people to communicate effectively. Remember, dog training is not about dogs: it is about people. How much patience someone has is directly linked to the success of their dog training. Using CPR, I want dog owners to see training as an opportunity to improve themselves as much as their dogs. When we achieve positive results with our dogs, it is a reflection of our effective communication, our patience and our empathy. Doesn't that make us better people?

The virtues of patience

There is a reason why patience is so virtuous. It is something that is developed over a lifetime. It is partly biological and partly learned, and while some pick it up quickly, for others, ironically, it requires its own amount of patience.

If we look at wild animals, we tend to assess their behaviour on survival adaptations such as hunting prowess, camouflage or mating rituals. Rarely do you see an animal documentary on the art of patience. But studies on everything from mice to chimpanzees have shown that some animals will delay gratification and wait prolonged periods to receive more valuable rewards.

With dogs, we see a mind capable of extraordinary control. A mind that yearns for direction and support to bring out the virtues that we love so much about them – virtues that brought us together all those millennia ago when our ancestors first adopted wolves as their own.

But dogs aren't inherently patient. I see puppies who have a whole new world in front of them, exploring and discovering at every waking moment. Puppies have not learnt the virtues of patience yet, instead they instinctively focus on how to manipulate and acquire resources quicker and on their terms.

Patience can be taught however and it is imperative that puppies begin learning the importance of it in a human world as early as possible. As I write this, I see Chester in my right peripheral vision. He has made a couple of undemanding whimpers and after having stood there at my side for the past half hour, I accept he has well and truly learnt the art of patience. Excuse me, I will be back in a moment – Chester is ready for his dinner.

He learnt this trait through my own consistent patience. We have worked together as a team where I have shown him that if he waits, he will get twice as much later on. This is what researchers call an intertemporal choice. Initially, dogs don't understand the benefits of this choice, instead lunging for the good stuff straight away. But leaders who themselves embody this virtue have the capacity to pay it forward on to others. Patience in dogs is indeed possible. But it starts with you.

For all its merits, patience is still a finite resource and while I appreciate Chester's willingness to wait for his dinner with extraordinary patience, at some point, he will blast me with an almighty jump if I don't respect his end of the bargain.

Let's practise patience in 10 steps

The best way to encourage your dog to be patient is to gradually increase the amount of time they wait for what they want, and reward each progression. Likened to impulse control, patience needs to be reinforced in small increments, building up to longer and longer periods of time. So let's start by identifying something your dog wants and then set them up for success.

For this exercise we will use the reward of coming inside the house.

1. Allow your dog to go outside. Don't enforce this, pick a time in which she wants to go outside.
2. When she returns to the door to come back inside, go to the door and allow her in immediately.
3. Repeat step 1 and when she returns to the door approach her and ask her to sit. If she volunteers to sit, that is much better, so allow her inside immediately.
4. Repeat step 1 and when she returns to the door approach her and wait for her to sit. Allow her inside within a second of her sitting.
5. Repeat step 1 and when she returns to the door, approach her within five seconds and wait for her to sit. Allow her inside within five seconds. Remember to really praise her and perhaps even offer a treat for her patience.
6. Repeat step 1 and when she returns to the door approach her within fifteen seconds and wait for her to sit. Allow her inside within fifteen seconds. Remember to really praise her and give her twice as many treats for getting to this stage without barking or scratching at the door. Repeat this step several times if you need to.
7. Repeat step 1 and when she returns to the door approach her within thirty seconds. She may have already sat by this time, so allow her inside immediately. Repeat this several times if you need to.
8. Repeat step 1 and when she returns to the door approach her within one minute. She may have sat

by this time, so allow her inside immediately. If she hasn't, wait for her to sit and allow her inside. By this stage, your dog should be learning that patience gets her what she wants and maybe even more. So be willing to offer her treats and praise to help her on the learning journey.

9. Repeat step 1 and when she returns to the door approach her within two minutes. She should be automatically sitting by now, so allow her in and praise. Repeat this several times if you need to.
10. Repeat step 1 and when she returns to the door approach her within five minutes.

Don't push her past five minutes if you don't have to. If she needs to stay outside for a longer period of time, then continue this method by giving her something positive to focus on outside. Treat dispensers with roasted chicken (free range) work really well. Keep an eye on her so that when she has finished and returns to the door, you can implement the training you have been working on with her.

Important to note! If your dog seems unsettled outside and looks as though she is going to begin barking or scratching, you have progressed further than she can cope. Go back a few steps and try again. Remember to set her up for success and be patient. Her patience needs to come from yours.

Whilst we may be teaching our dogs patience in this exercise, we are also teaching them many other things including, self control, predictability, trust and respect.

A dog who trusts and respects you in any situation rarely displays destructive behaviours.

These ten simple steps are an example of how you can teach your dog to be patient, whilst showing them that they can have what they want if they wait. Teaching patience in your dog is so valuable to them, because it helps them learn to deal with the human world, which will inevitably require their patience here and there. Dogs who are patient are generally more calm, cooperative and controlled.

RESPECT

Each and every day, we are confronted with a range of social dynamics. Sometimes these interactions are positive, sometimes they aren't. During our daily social journey it is easy to focus on other's reactions to us. However, most of the time, people's perception of us is unrelated to who we are and what we do. It is a reflection of their own inner sense of respect, or lack thereof.

Dogs are great teachers of respect. They let you know immediately if they respect you or not. They do this in their behaviour and body language. Dogs who perceive their owners as positive leaders will show this by listening to them and looking to them in times of uncertainty.

Respectful dogs will come when they are called or, better yet, come when they are not called. They will offer to sit for you when they want to be acknowledged and they will wait patiently because they know you will cooperate. When your dog respects you, you know that you have earned it. I don't think there is any other species on earth who makes you earn their respect like a dog does. And, only when we treat our dogs with respect can we expect it to be returned.

Just when we thought dogs couldn't be any more esteemed, we discover that they are even capable of dismissing those in our lives who do not treat us with the respect they believe we deserve. Research conducted in Tokyo studied several dogs' reactions to a person who displayed unhelpful or unkind interactions with their owner compared to a person who did not interact with their owner at all. Results showed that dogs are far less likely to take food from the disrespectful person over the neutral person, suggesting that our best friends feel contemptuous towards people who are not willing to contribute positively to our lives.

I would argue that studies like these may be an appeal to nature fallacy, in which clearly we want our dogs to be our protectors so we look for answers to questions that confirm the unbreakable bond we share. Dogs who are less likely to take food from 'mean' people may have assessed their uncooperative behaviour and made a judgment on whether they could trust that person for themselves. The dog may be wondering *Is that food safe?* or *Is this person a threat to me?* The dog may be just as concerned about their own wellbeing as they are about yours.

Whilst I make this point, I do still believe that the relationship between man and dog is something incredibly special. And though we tend to anthropomorphise them, the bond we share remains, in my opinion, one that is unique. I'd snub a thousand people before I'd snub a dog. Why? Because I know that a dog is always going to see the real me, and I know that they will always respectfully show me the same.

In the next chapter, we're going to look more closely at the vital role that respect – and, by virtue, trust – plays in your relationship with your dog.

According to the Oxford Dictionary, respect is defined as *having due regard for the feelings, wishes or rights of another.* It is also defined as having *deep admiration for someone or something for their their abilities, qualities, or achievements.*

Respect is a weighted word that threads prominently

through our personal journeys in life. It affects who we meet, what we do and who we are. It is not just about who we admire, but what we admire most in ourselves and who we want to be. So, can we have positive relationships with others if our internal relationships are negative? I don't believe we can. I see people who suffer from insecurities each day in my work, who engage in unhealthy and dysfunctional relationships because they do not have a healthy relationship within themselves. Sadly, these unhealthy relationships extend to those with their dogs too.

I often see owners objectify their dogs and speak of them with ill regard. There is clearly an issue with how people treat animals in this country and I believe it's a reflection of their own lack of self worth. Over 60 000 cruelty cases were reported to the RSCPA in 2015 alone, with only 263 of these resulting in successful prosecution. Neglect and torture are the most common causes of cruelty in Australia, with cats and dogs suffering the most.

Whilst there is no evidence of causation, the link between animal cruelty and other violence is correlated. In America, 70 per cent of human–human violent crimes were carried out by people who had previously been abusive towards their pets or other animals.

Cruelty is a whole new, darker level of disrespect, but clearly there is a stepping stone between those who do not respect animals and those who are cruel. It's a complicated relationship these people have with themselves. Some may be inherently evil, some may be transitioning from lighter shades to dark, but most are just self-contemptuous. Rather than disempowering those who struggle to connect with animals, I want to deal with the cause of the problem: the underlying lack of respect so many people have for themselves.

At some point in all of our lives, our sense of self-respect is challenged. Sadly, very little in this modern, mass-media world actually promotes self-respect. There is not a corner to turn without a billboard telling you to change. So how can you experience inner self-admiration when the modern world doesn't want you to?

You can by realising that you are a miracle. You are alive against all odds on this planet. The chance of you being born is one in four trillion. One in four trillion! You have had to endure and overcome illness, disease, daily threats and, still, you are here reading this book and focusing on how to improve your already miraculous life! You are a phenomenon. Don't spend your life wishing to be something you aren't. *Be yourself,* they say, *as everyone else is taken*. Find who you are and admire it. Believe in it. Become it.

Look at your dog now and you will see someone who needs you to believe in yourself. You are their guardian, their leader and the centre of their existence. When you find internal respect, you gain external respect. How you feel about yourself deep down affects those around you, including your dog. They are a reflection of you.

So take care of yourself first.

LET'S BE PRACTICAL IN 3, 2, 1 . . .

The Consistency, Patience and Respect approach is useful for you, your family and your dog. So each day, find a time to practise this healthy pattern of living. Grab a pen and paper, or your phone and write down the three headings below. Then brainstorm how CPR is going to help you in your life via the 3-2-1 approach.

Three things I will be consistent with every day

1. e.g. being on time at work
2.
3.

Follow through with these actions and watch others around you respond. You will see your dog feels more relaxed, and your partner and children feel more positive, because you are taking control of something that makes your life a little easier in the long run.

Two things I will be more patient about each day

1. e.g. helping my son with his homework
2.

Slow down, take a deep breath and take the time to do something properly.

One way I will respect myself each day

1. e.g. remembering I am number one

Nobody can look after others, including their dog, if they can't look after themselves. You must take the time to consistently and patiently do something for yourself every day. For me, I take five minutes out of my day, to find somewhere quiet and focus on just me and nothing else for that time. I start my day slower but more efficiently. My mind is positive and those around me can feel and benefit from this.

Did you know . . . *there are more than three hundred dog breeds across the world? Among those there are ancient breeds, genetically divergent from modern dogs such as pugs. These include dogs such as the akita, chow chow, malamute, Afghan hound, dingo, husky and of course the greyhound. Interestingly, it's thought that the name greyhound came from improperly pronouncing the German word Greishund, which means ancient dog.*

4.

Trust and Respect

'Nothing is more despicable than respect based on fear.'

Albert Camus

Trust and respect are virtues of leadership that can only ever be earned. Dogs will only follow a person they don't trust or respect through fear or obligation. So, when your dog chooses to cooperate with you, listens to you and follows your guidance voluntarily, they are telling you something very important. They are telling you that they believe in you. They are telling you that you are a leader.

Although we may overly anthropomorphise our dogs (assigning them the same traits and feelings that humans exhibit), it cannot be denied that dogs experience many similar emotions to us. So even though they may not feel and think exactly as we do, they still feel and think.

It makes me think of the biblical proverb, 'Do to others as you would have them do to you.' We see this mandate appear across almost every religion throughout history. Perhaps the earliest recorded example of this comes from around 2000 BC in an ancient Egyptian story called *The Eloquent Peasant*. In this ancient story, the golden rule or moral to the story was, 'Now this is the command, do to the doer to make him do.' This concept was personified in the goddess Ma'at, who embodied harmony, morality and justice, and was the representation of how Egyptians were expected to live.

Confucius, the Chinese philosopher, educator and politician who lived around 500 BC, also imparted a similar concept through his teachings. He lived with a strong emphasis on morality, loyalty and respect, including the proverb, 'Never impose on others what you would not choose for yourself.' There is no doubt that across history, the importance of compassion, empathy, and love for one another has universally been a major focus for the evolution of us as a civilised species.

Sadly, however, disrespect and mistrust have also been evident in human behaviour for many millennia. People throughout history have endured countless instances of violence and war among their own kind.

Looking back at history, it was not that long ago that people experimented brutally on others in an attempt to understand them better. From drowning women to see if they were witches, to attempting to scare the mental illness out of people by putting them in snake pits, our attempts to discard those who did not conform to the norm was undeniably cruel. Even more recently, the Stanford Prison Experiment of the 1970s highlighted a disturbing truth about human nature, revealing that we are perhaps not as civilised as we might like to think. Psychologist Philip Zimbardo led a behavioural experiment in the basement of the university department, whereby a group of undergraduate volunteers were assigned roles as either guards or prisoners and the behaviours in their new roles were observed and documented. The experiment was terminated early because many subjects who had adopted and embodied the role of prison guard engaged in sadistic behaviour, causing intense emotional trauma to the inmate subjects. While current psychological testing undergoes much more rigorous ethical oversight, the results from this experiment present evidence that many humans in a position of power are likely to impose physical and emotional torture to reinforce their status.

This makes me think a lot of how we have experimented with dog training, using methods that only partially work, regardless of whether there is any science to support them. In fact, we have done exactly the same as what we have done with people in the past: letting our beliefs or fears affect how we train a dog and how we treat them, when all along there was a much kinder way. Now we know better, moral treatment in dog training is something that should be across the board and the first point of call in any behaviour training. Dignity, kindness and respect should come first with your dog, as it should for any relationship.

Over time, many trainers have talked about respect as an essential pillar of training, but only recently have we actually understood exactly what it truly means.

Historically, respect was one sided. It was about teaching the dog to respect you through discipline, boundaries and harsh consequences. If a dog did not obey, then they were being disrespectful of your authority and as a consequence were punished until they started to show 'respect'.

I grew up with this training philosophy, as I am sure many of you did. I believed that dogs were there to do as you said and if they didn't, then there was something wrong with the dog. Perhaps they weren't smart enough or it was because of the breed, or they were the wrong dog for a family. The truth is that people still practise this method and believe in the underlying philosophy. They don't realise that if a dog doesn't do as they say, most likely there is something wrong with the training approach, not the dog. The authoritarian method is not about respect. Although it teaches the dog to comply, it is not out of respect, but out of appeasement and often fear. A dog is a reflection of us and if they are compliant out of fear, then what does that say about us and our relationship with them? Have you earned anything positive in that relationship or have you merely achieved results through enforcement, domination and fear?

The relationship we have with others ultimately comes down to one thing: us. At some point, we need to look from within at what's outside. An example of how your emotional state can affect your perception of reality is Sarah and her severe phobia of two dogs.

CASE STUDY

Sarah had a phobia of dogs, so much so that she would avoid walking down her street to get to the bus stop past the dogs who barked at her. She would get in her car, drive down the street, park at the end of the road and then get on the bus. She felt threatened by the dogs who would bark at her as she walked past them. She felt that these dogs hated her. She felt vulnerable, disliked, anxious and fearful.

Sarah was genuinely petrified of these dogs. It had affected her life so much that she began to avoid day-to-day tasks, such as putting the washing out on the line, for fear that the dog on the other side of the fence would break through and attack her.

Sarah did not feel any personal contempt towards any dog and didn't understand why they would hate her so much and want to hurt her. She couldn't understand why it was that if she could respect them, they could not respect her back.

I met Sarah after she had suffered from this life-changing

fear for months and could no longer even leave the house. She talked to no end about these dogs. She described how dangerous they were, how everybody hated them and how she was even considering moving because of them. I listened with patience and respect for her feelings.

Once Sarah was exhausted from the emotional distress of talking about it, I asked her one question: 'How do you feel about yourself right now?'

Sarah broke down to tears. I let her cry.

She told me that she was frustrated and depressed as her partner had just left her. She was struggling to get out of bed and go to work each morning and felt so insecure within herself that she didn't really want to engage with anything anymore. Without prompting, she continued on to talk about the dogs, who she was genuinely scared of, but perhaps were her scapegoat for feeling the way she was and why she behaved the way she did. I let Sarah talk for over an hour about her past, her present and her future. It was clear that these dogs were not the cause of her anxiety, her own sense of worthlessness was.

We met the dogs that day. One was a German shepherd and the other a Maltese–Shih tzu cross. These dogs spent much of their time together, sometimes fourteen hours a day. We stood across the road from them, Sarah trembling with inconsolable fear. But to me it was clear that they were just as frustrated and anxious as she was.

The two dogs eventually stopped barking and came up to the fence. Their ears fell back, their tails relaxed, and I explained to Sarah that she shared a lot in common with them. They weren't targeting her. They didn't dislike her. They didn't think she was a bad person. They were simply expressing their own internal state indiscriminately each and every day. I knew it was safe to approach the dogs and so I took Sarah by the hand and stepped up to the fence. The tags on their collars read Daisy and Milly and as we walked towards them, their body language diffused from frustration to curiosity and excitement. Both dogs gently took the food I had in my hand and the four of us sat together until the treats had all been gobbled up. Sarah gave the shepherd, Milly, a scratch under the chin as a peace offering, which Milly accepted by moving closer for more.

We walked home and Sarah was clearly elated. She had faced her fear and all along, her fear had nothing to do with the dogs. She told me how she felt, that she was proud of herself and she recognised that how she felt inside was redirected onto others. I told her that life is full of metaphorically barking dogs. There are people in our lives who let us down and who disregard our thoughts and feelings each and every day.

Who you are is only determined by who you think you are. Find the good. There is so much of it. Barking dogs will always bark, no matter who you are, but remember that the bark is never directed at you, rather it is a manifestation of the dog's own internal unease.

Respect yourself. Respect others regardless of whether they reciprocate. You never know what sort of day that barking dog is having. We never truly know the struggles they face in their lives each day. Treating others well comes from our own emotional care and love for ourselves. The better we feel about ourselves, the better the world becomes around us.

Dog owners who are themselves the proverbial barking dogs, are commonly insolent toward others. I think that at some stage in all our lives we feel that growl within us. But those who experience the relentless growl within them must stop and start to look inside. Not just for their own wellbeing but also for those they love.

TRUST

Many years ago, I failed my dog Chester. We visited a spot on the beautiful Mornington Peninsula one summer day – it was and still is his favourite place in the world. At this particular bay beach, the tide goes so far out it meets the horizon and Chester can bound through the tiny waves getting nothing more than his toes and knees wet. He is confident and in complete control. I throw bits of driftwood that we find together on the shore and he leaps like a hefty gazelle porpoising through the shallow water, anticipating the exact spot it will land when I throw it. There is something so pure and uplifting seeing someone you love so happy. In that moment, there is nothing more he could want and, in all honesty, there is nothing more I could want either.

On that day, Chester and I lunched on the rocks, but as we rested, the tide awakened. The water began to rise, as did the waves, and we found ourselves marooned twenty metres from the shore. While the water reached just above my waist and I was able to walk back to the sand, Chester would either have to be carried or he'd have to swim. He'd never swum before. Although he'd look like he wanted to so many times, the water never reached higher than the base of his nose before he'd quickly move back to a more comfortable depth.

This day, I made a decision for him, regardless of how he felt or what he wanted, I pushed him in. With a great splash, every inch of Chester's body propelled for dear life as he tried to keep his head above water. In a panic, he paddled over to me and proceeded to climb up my body in a frenzy. It worked. I grabbed each side of his body while his claws dug into my chest for grip and I carried him back to shore. To this day, I still have scars on my chest, a reminder of the mistake that for months destroyed the trust Chester had for me near water.

Nowadays, Chester still loves the beach more than anything, but the base of his nose remains the highest point his body is ever exposed to water. And that's okay. I would much rather have his trust than have him swim out of fear or obligation. That's the thing about trust: it needs to be mutual to work. It involves mutual compromise, empathy and respect. While we may trust someone else, without their trust, the relationship is doomed. It's the same for our dogs. Without mutual trust, neither of you will ever be able to reach the full potential of that relationship.

Considering how another person or animal feels helps us build trust in a relationship. Respecting their beliefs, their desires and their fears is so important. Communicating that you will never intentionally hurt them and that you will always behave in a way that is in their best interests makes you someone to be trusted. In its mutuality, a relationship based on trust and respect is the most successful, fulfilling engagement possible. I believe it is what we all yearn for deep down in our soul. Your dog deserves this and so do you.

So how do we practically develop this relationship together? The first step is to identify what it is that's important to you and what it is that's important to your dog. Write down what you believe is important to you in your relationships. Then, write down what you think is important to your dog in his relationships. Listed here are examples of the things you may like to record:

YOU	YOUR DOG
Trust	Trust
Respect	Respect

Shared values	Consistency
Compassion	Patience
Equality	Resources
Reliability	Reliability
Compromise	Compromise

You may add to or delete from this list. But it is important to create it, to think about it and to work on it. You'll see from my list that my dogs and I want many similar things in our relationships. The two lists deviate because I have more control than my dogs do. Because of this, we are in many ways more responsible for the successful relationship with our dogs than they are themselves.

Keep the table you create in your mind as well as on paper to refer to later. You will see trust and respect are threaded throughout this book because these two words are undoubtedly the life force of any successful relationship.

HOW TO MAINTAIN TRUST WITH YOUR DOG

Let's examine the issue of trust through a commonly accepted training method. When you're raising a puppy, many dog trainers will instruct you to take food away from them whilst they are eating. This is intended to teach the puppy not to become aggressive during feeding time.

In every interaction with your dog, it is important to consider whether or not you are building or breaking trust and respect. Let's think logically. Resources such as food are important to our dogs, so removing their food is understandably a threat. But what if we give it straight back, won't they become desensitised to the action? My answer is that maybe they will, maybe they won't. Is that a risk worth taking?

Just like us, dogs all have unique personalities. Even within breeds and between siblings we see different individuals, with different nose prints and different temperaments. While repeatedly taking food away from one dog may never affect their behaviour, taking food away from another may result in an irreversible breakdown of trust and respect. And a big bite!

Many people think that removing food from a dog is about teaching them to be respectful and teaching them who's boss and who controls the resources. But the truth is, you are always controlling the resources anyway. You are the one each day who decides to fill up the bowl and give it to your dog. This never needs to be a power struggle. Clearly, you are always the one in charge, not your dog.

CASE STUDY

I was called out to a couple's home once to help them with their golden retriever, let's call him Bitey. The couple, Jo and Ross, had bought Bitey from a pet store just six months prior and clearly adored him. They had bought the 'how to raise a puppy right' books that day, chosen a matching collar and lead, selected the baby-blue-coloured bedding and left with an oversized bag of puppy kibble. These are the things you need to think about when you get a puppy, right? Of course they are, but they are the no-brainers.

When Bitey came home, his dedicated owners began to apply their new knowledge and it began with his food bowl. The first cup of kibble was vigorously thrown in the bowl and carefully placed in the kitchen. Bitey gobbled it up in five seconds and returned to them wanting more. Those adoring brown eyes, the clumsy gait and manipulative head tilt melted their hearts, so out came another cup. This time, Jo and Ross decided to try what they had been reading. They placed the bowl down on the floor and knelt beside it. They held their hands up so he couldn't reach it and waited for him to sit. He sat eventually and as soon as he finished his first mouthful, the bowl was swiftly removed. Again, Bitey was cued to sit and wait before he could have his next mouthful. On the third attempt, Bitey predicted the behaviours of his new owners and growled. He was immediately scolded, finished chewing his last mouthful and was put into the laundry.

The next morning, at feeding time, Bitey and his owners all rushed to the kitchen, all with a clear association of it as a place where resources are provided. The owners anxiously filled the cup with kibble and emptied it into the bowl, asking Bitey to sit and wait. Bitey sat, waiting patiently for what no doubt seemed an eternity as his owners counted the ten seconds that their training book had told them to. At last the bowl was placed down and Bitey proceeded to take the first mouthful. As his owners knelt down to repeat the same agonising ritual from the night therefore, Bitey not only growled but he leapt up and bit Jo on her hand. With all three in shock, Bitey ran off, piddled in his bed and tried to hide under it. From that day, Bitey would not only avoid any metal bowls, he would growl and snap if anyone came within five metres of him eating.

After they had finished telling me this story, I told them another. It was a story from Bitey's point of view. This is what Bitey would say:

> *Food is an important resource to me and I work hard to get it from you. I sit and I wait but you still take it away from me. I feel anxious and confused not being able to predict or control when my food is here and when it is not. I feel protective of it now and growl because that is the only way I can feel in control. I have tried to tell you how I feel, but you haven't heard me.*

Please start listening to me, just as I am expected to listen to you.

I then gave Jo a fifty-dollar note, telling her it was a refund for the deposit they had made for the session. She held it in her hand, a little confused, but accepted it and proceeded to put it in her pocket. Before her hand could reach down, I grabbed the money from her and said, 'Oh no sorry, my mistake, that's actually my money.' Shocked and taken aback, Jo accepted the mistake and I continued talking about Bitey.

Seconds later, I gave the money back to Jo in complete apology for my mistake, that it was actually hers, that I had made an embarrassing mistake and I dangled the note in front of her. Again, Jo reluctantly and slowly took the money back, unsure of what I was going to do next. Of course, I ripped it from her hands again and both Ross and Jo began to see what point I was making. I asked Jo how she felt, to which she admitted she was quite anxious and unnerved by the sight of the fifty-dollar note. I asked her if she still wanted it and of course she said yes, in fact she wanted it more than ever. I then asked her if she trusted me. Both Ross and Jo together sighed and said, 'No.'

It was clear to them now where they went wrong. They had unknowingly lost invaluable trust and respect from their puppy, all within a space of minutes. It's so easy to do.

I never took my dog Chester's bowl from him. In fact, I don't think I have ever taken food away from him, unless what was in his mouth was harmful. If he is asked to 'give' – an instruction to open his mouth and drop whatever he has on the ground – then he knows that I may have something ten times better for him. Sometimes I do, sometimes I don't, but he understands that when I take something from his mouth, there is good reason for it. Relationships are not about dominance. They are about mutual trust and respect.

SUMMARY

Trust and respect are never one-sided in a successful relationship. A mutual regard for the other is essential, but at the same time, it is important we feel this for ourselves first. Without self-respect and trust, we fall vulnerable to those outside our family circle, who redirect their own self-contempt onto us. Or, we end up taking part in the bullying behaviours ourselves. Be kind to yourself and others. Be the person your dog needs you to be.

Did you know . . . *according to the RSPCA, in the 2015/16 financial year, over 62 000 animal cruelty complaints were investigated? That's an increase of almost 2000 investigations from the previous financial year and close to double the amount ten years prior. Are we getting more cruel? Or are we simply investigating more and more?*

5.

Empathy

Empathy: the ability to understand and share the feelings of another.

As humans, being aware of others' feelings is one of the traits we have developed to coexist peacefully with each other. Research shows that there is, unsurprisingly, a positive correlation between how much empathy someone has and how willing they are to help others.

Across the history of civilisation, empathy is clearly an advantage to the socialisation and survival of communal species, including people and dogs.

But what about those outside of our community? Do we care as much for them? Some argue that while empathy has survival advantages between individuals who are close, it does not necessarily benefit the greater good. They believe that empathy is subjective and that people can only connect with those they are emotionally invested in. For instance, we tend to care more about mammals who are furry than lizards who are scaly and we are more inclined to help attractive people over the less physically advantaged. We are intrinsically looking to connect with those we can relate to and those who we perceive are successful in life. The more connected we are, the more empathy we display.

Empathy-sceptic and Yale professor Paul Bloom makes an interesting argument about how being so connected to others' emotions can also be exhausting. Those who display a more empathic nature are generally more emotional and sensitive people, and thus more prone to depression and anxiety. Such people are more easily hurt, prefer moments of solitude to overcrowded environments and can intuit the energy and feelings of others. No wonder the world appears to be less and less empathic!

EMOTIONAL EMPATHY VERSUS COGNITIVE EMPATHY

In the *Boston Review*, Professor Bloom stated that being a good person is 'more related to a distanced compassion, along with self-control and a sense of justice'. This is more of a 'cognitive' (a logical and balanced approach) empathy and I do think that this approach is a far more sustainable way of being a good person – not just for others, but for yourself as well.

I have made a conscious effort to live more with a cognitive appreciation of empathy. By this, I mean having an understanding of others' feelings and emotions without actually experiencing those feelings and emotions myself. So I got to thinking, on reflection of all the literature around empathy, perhaps the best way to care for others is through a distanced and detached viewpoint, as Bloom described. This way, we are able to care for others whilst preserving our own emotional wellbeing.

Of course, for those in our lives that we are personally connected to and invested in, having emotional empathy remains inescapable. The important part is being able to decipher what deserves our emotional empathy and what deserves our cognitive empathy. It's a little like the serenity prayer: 'Give me the serenity to accept the things I cannot change, the courage to change the things I can and the wisdom to know the difference.' So I guess saving the world is off the to-do list then?

I really do believe we can change the world. And we are. I believe we can, partly because I have lived most of my life being told I couldn't, and wanted to prove people wrong, but also because I realised that when we have a clear head and resist being drawn into the stress and emotional vortex of the world, we can do great things! Those who are passionate change-makers are the ones who persistently fight for what they believe in. Not with fists or emotions, but with the strength of a cognitive empathic mind. So, what are you passionate about?

For me, animal welfare tops the list. Imagine if everyone in the world did not suffer. Imagine if we lived in a fairy tale, where everything was inherently good. Where all animals, including humans, lived a life of peace and tranquillity, never encountering harm. Bluebirds chirped on your shoulder and you sang together in harmony whilst picking wild flowers in the meadow. Perhaps I've digressed? This imagery is misleading and dysfunctional however and it's called the 'appeal to nature' fallacy. In reality, suffering exists across all life forms, in some way or another. For as long as there is life on earth, so too will there be suffering. But Mother Nature, as cruel as she may be, is equally beautiful. The bluebirds will always sing and the flowers continue to bloom in the meadows. Which side you see of Mother Nature depends on which side you choose look at.

We can still change the world and minimise the world's suffering, if we empower and educate those around us, leading by example. That's the thing about leadership, those who follow choose to because they believe in you. When I think of what I am passionate about, all I can hope for is that someone out there is following me or, even better, someone is walking beside me in support of the values I am fighting for. Imagine if we all walked together.

CASE STUDY

Note: Any reactive or aggressive behavioural issues should always be managed in consultation with a qualified dog behaviourist.

I once met a woman named Emma who had rescued a young border collie, Jet, and had called me because he was 'aggressive'. Each day she would take Jet down to the local park and invariably Jet would get into a fight. She explained to me that this new dog had come from a farm and was the only one in the litter who had survived.

Months earlier, Emma had taken Jet to the park for the first time. For Jet, it was overwhelming. He immediately ran toward the dogs in the centre of the oval and began relentlessly chasing them, barking at them and clearly antagonising them. Some may say he was herding.

Those who are lucky enough to be challenged by the remarkable mind and energy of a working dog will no doubt be nodding their heads in recognition. While I believe all dogs are individuals, regardless of breed, there can be no doubt that the border collie is predisposed to herd. A working dog inherently desires purpose. And while I strongly believe all dogs yearn for purpose, the collie in particular benefits in health and happiness when in a position of utility. If these dogs lack purpose they will become frustrated. Their owners will become equally frustrated – by the destructive behaviour their dog exhibits in their backyard.

While most other dogs in the park were able to tolerate this newcomer's unsociable quirks, one dog didn't. As Jet pushed his limits, this dog reared his body up and took to Jet as if he were a squeaky toy. Jet was pinned down and after several attempts by the owners to extinguish the fight, the dogs eventually tired and Jet was pulled away. Jet was yelled at, as the emotional chaos within Emma was redirected onto her dog. She yelled at him whilst yanking his collar in a combination of humiliation and frustration. Once she had calmed, they both went home. And whilst Emma had eventually overcome the anxiety, Jet was still unnerved by the incident, more anxious than ever.

The next day, Emma and Jet returned to the same park, this time with Jet on-lead. Co-tethered, they approached the middle of the oval, where the same dog was and, once again, both animals expressed their anxious contempt for one another. Jet and the larger dog fought with more gusto than the day before, until blood, sweat and tears laced across all who were intertwined in the chaos. Emma had tried to do the right thing. She tried to get back on the proverbial horse and help Jet face his fears. She was applying a logical solution. But what was logical to Jet?

From Jet's perspective, this dog was a threat. Nothing had been resolved between the two dogs and, worse still, Jet was tethered to his owner, leaving him with no control. Our logic compared to a dog's is often very different. But while there are clear differences in our outlooks, only one of us has the capacity to view both sides of the story. That comes down to you.

If we are going to be able to provide happy and healthy lives for our dogs, we must think from their perspective. Applying empathy helps us to understand how they are feeling and what they are thinking. We must always act on what they need at the time. For Jet, he needed to learn how to interact safely with other dogs and he needed leadership from someone who understood where he was coming from. I helped Emma achieve this for Jet, through applying cognitive empathy in a practical sense.

First and foremost, Emma needed to regain trust from Jet, so we embarked on implementing CPR and teaching her how to capture the calm, cooperative and controlled within him. Each time he displayed these behaviours or mindsets, Emma rewarded him with praise, treats and safety. Once trust was two directional, we returned to the park and started from scratch.

Emma, Jet and I began at a distance from the centre of the park where the dogs were. I identified that Jet had two motivations at the park, one was play and the other was safety. So we began to play with his favourite ball, along with some hide and seek, allowing him to focus on positive interactions with Emma, without being confronted with danger from other dogs. Emma had conditioned Jet to learn that the words 'let's play' meant it was game time, and so every time he saw a dog in the distance, Emma exclaimed, 'Let's play!'

Sighting dogs started to take on a whole different meaning to Jet. Dogs meant focus and play with his owner, in safety, not threats or danger. Over time, Emma became more comfortable, and allowed well socialised dogs a little closer to Jet, remembering she could always get his attention with her invitation to play. A month went by and Jet was able to play with a select group of dogs who were regular attendees at the park. They found another spot to engage in daily fun and Emma reports that Jet has two besties; one is another working dog and the other, a pug called Darryl.

Whilst off-lead dog parks can provide space and engagement for many dogs each and every day, they are spaces to enter with caution. Always sit on the sideline and watch the dynamics of the dogs interacting. Are there dogs trying to get away from others? Are there dogs cornering or pestering other dogs? Are there dogs persistently jumping up on their owners or hiding behind them? Are there growls or scraps here and there? Enter at any of these times and you are most likely setting your dog up for failure.

If you have a dog who is for whatever reason nervous around other dogs, then remember CPR. Remember the importance of mutual trust and respect and how important it is for you to think from your dog's point of view. When this is fluent, your dog's behaviour changes because their emotional state settles.

PRACTICAL STEPS FOR IMPLEMENTING CPR

Step 1

Observe your dog right now. What are they doing? How are they feeling? Can you read their emotional state? Write down their feelings from their perspective.

Start with, 'My name is [insert your dog's name] and I am feeling . . .'

For my dog Chester right now, he is standing beside me, staring at me with his head positioned low. I know exactly what he wants. He wants two things. Firstly, he wants food, and secondly he wants to go for a run in the reserve across the road. No, actually, he wants three things. He wants food, then he wants to go for a run in the reserve across the road, then he wants food again! How do I know this? Because if I were to get up and follow him, he would take me straight to the fridge and sit. If I were to feed him, he would then take me to the laundry where the doggy door is and stand there, waiting to go for a run. He clearly tells me how he is feeling and what he wants all the time, as best he can. It is my job to listen. This doesn't mean that I give in to his wishes all the time, but it's important that I can understand what he wants.

Step 2

Each day, write down on a pad or as a note in your phone what your dog is doing.

How long for: 2 minutes at a time
When: 3-6 times a day
Duration: A week

For example, start to observe them when you are getting ready for a walk, at a park, tying them up before you go into a shop, or preparing their dinner. How are they feeling at that time? Are you listening to them? There will be a range of behaviours you will write down that you may have never considered that will give you an understanding of their emotional state.

Using Chester as an example again, I know that he can be anxious when larger dogs approach him and attempt to invade his personal space. I see it in his body as it stiffens.

I see it in the white of his eye and how his entire being freezes as he waits to find out the motivations of the other dog. I know that he is uncomfortable in those moments. Once that short but seemingly interminable moment ends, he shakes his body, runs ahead and spins around 180 degrees, landing in a play bow towards the lanky pointer he met only seconds ago.

It's okay for your dog to be uncertain sometimes, we all are. But it is important that in that time of uncertainty, you have their back. In instances in which I am not sure of the other dog's motivations, I encourage Chester away from the situation with yummy treats well before I think it may end badly. I am constantly reading him, reading others and setting him up for success.

But my dog is out of control! you may think. I can say with absolute confidence that if you have a dog who you cannot control, it is because you have not practised CPR. That is, you have not *consistently*, *patiently* and *respectfully* listened to them, acted in their best interests and set them up for success.

'But I have a dominant dog!' you may respond. In truth, your dog is not dominant over you. Instead, dominant behaviour of a dog towards a person is a direct reflection of the relationship between the two.

Does your dog respect you? Do they trust you? If they did, they would not be displaying 'dominant' demanding behaviours. This is not a reflection of the dog, but the person on the other end of the leash.

Step 3

Start to identify the behaviours your dog is displaying and the emotional state that may accompany it. For example:

Behaviour	Emotional state
Yawning	Anxiety, nervousness, excitement
Body shaking	Anxiety, nervousness, excitement
Tail between legs	Fear, anxiety, need to avoid or escape
Panting	Anxiety, uncertainty
Licking lips	Attempt to smell better, or an expression of anxiety
Pulling on lead	A need to control/lack of impulse control
Jumping up on you	Anxiety, nervousness, excitement, lack of self-control, learned behaviour reinforced by you
Mounting a dog	Displaced anxiety or excitability
Snapping/growling at another dog	Fear, defensive/offensive reaction, frustration, anxiety

When you see negative behaviours and you understand why your dog is behaving this way, this is when you need to act and lead. Better yet, when you can predict these behaviours are going to occur, it is your job to act then, preventing any negative response or behaviour.

If your dog is showing signs of anxiety, and you didn't predict it, then learn how to control the environment and remove what is causing the anxiety. For example, if your dog is showing signs of fear as a dog approaches, do a U-turn, trot away and make it fun. Identify the threshold (the distance at which your dog can't tolerate any more) and *consistently*, *patiently* and *respectfully* aim never to surpass it.

CAN DOGS HAVE EMPATHY?

Empathy was thought to be unique in humans for a very long time. However, chimpanzees have shown sympathetic behaviours by hugging and consoling each other during times of stress or loss, which is one of the building blocks of empathy and similar to how children display concern for others.

This got me to thinking about empathy. Chimpanzees are more likely to show these basic empathic behaviours towards those who were closest to them, such as family members or those who have supported them in times of distress. We cannot deny the emotional attachment we have to those we love and while we maintain a strong sense of justice for all, I believe it is near impossible to distance our compassion from those closest to us.

I will never forget hearing a story the ever-inspiring primatologist Dame Jane Goodall told years ago, when she reflected on a visit she made back to a group of chimpanzees after a prolonged absence. She had brought with her a particular food to offer to them on her return and upon the first moments of their welcomed reunion, she offered it to the alpha male. With her arm reached out and her hand open, Goodall presented this symbol of respect to him. How he responded, still to this day, sends shivers of awe down my spine.

This magnificent, distant relative of ours also reached out his arm and opened his hand on to Jane's, but instead of taking the food, he gently pressed her fingers back over it and respectfully pushed it back into her arms. What I took from the story was that she and this chimpanzee shared a great moment of mutual respect and trust, perhaps even empathy, where he sacrificed a valuable resource to consolidate a more valuable relationship.

Another way that chimpanzees (and humans) display empathy is through yawning. Called the 'yawn contagion', it is a behaviour that can be subconsciously 'caught' by another, where one animal's yawn elicits another's yawn and so on. It is thought that this contagious behaviour is a sign of connectedness and cohesion with one another. As Dutch primatologist and ethologist Frans de Waal described it: 'Yawning is a sort of proxy for empathy.' Over the past few decades, de Waal has been a champion of research into animal empathy, with his studies uncovering the parallels between mammals' capacity for cooperation, morality and fairness.

We had thought until fairly recently that only humans and the great apes yawned as a sign of empathy, but anecdotes from across the world have suggested that our dogs also exhibit the yawn contagion. Many people have reported yawning after they see their dog yawn, but, most interestingly, people have also reported that their dogs will yawn after they have. While more rigorous research is needed, it gives us a glimmer of hope that our best furry mates really do get us just as well as our own species, if not better.

BEING EMPATHIC WITH YOUR DOG

Empathy is the first stage of understanding how to train a dog. Your dog's unwanted behaviours are just a reflection of their emotional state. Becoming empathic towards your dog is such an incredible journey. You gain amazing insight into the life of another and learn how to consider that life from their point of view without imposing your expectations of them.

Have a look at the behaviours listed in the following table. Try not to look at the second and third columns. Read each behaviour and think about your dog. Ask yourself why a dog may exhibit these behaviours.

I have collected data from dog owners over many years,

analysed it, and have listed the most common causes for their dogs' unwanted behaviours.

Now, have a read of the second column, without uncovering the third. Can you identify with any of these?

After talking to thousands of people, I realised that how people felt was completely one-sided, focusing on how their dog's behaviour affected their own lives. But when I analysed the possible motivations of the dog, they tended to focus not on themselves, but on the relationship and their need to be a part of it.

UNWANTED BEHAVIOUR	**WHAT THE CLIENT OFTEN THINKS**	**WHAT'S THE REAL ISSUE?**
Digging up backyard	My dog is a bad dog	Is your dog bored? Are they looking for something to do? Are they trying to warm up or cool down? Digging holes is often an instinctive behaviour to help regulate body temperature. Are they suffering from separation anxiety?
Barking when left alone	My dog is trying to be disruptive (and driving the neighbours crazy!)	Your dog is calling out to you. They are barking or howling to communicate to their family, because being alone for prolonged periods is not natural for a social animal. Are they bored?

Urinating inside	My dog pees to spite me	Is your dog desexed? Male and female dogs instinctively and subconsciously mark their territory, particularly when they are in season. Is there a new dog in the home? Has something changed in the household to make them feel territorial? Is your dog elderly, with bladder control issues? Does your dog have dementia? Is your dog able to go outside when they need to? Do you have a consistent routine where your dog is able to get outside and relieve themselves regularly? Is your dog suffering from separation anxiety?
Growling, lunging at other dogs	I have an aggressive dog	Is your dog trying to protect itself? Are they trying to protect the family? Have they been attacked previously? Have you read the body language of the dog you are approaching? Perhaps that dog is giving signs of defensive/offensive behaviours. Have you set your dog up for success, by reading their body language and giving them something positive to experience during a time of stress, such as U-turn and treats? Are you setting your dog up to fail by continuing to approach the other dog?

Pulls on lead	My dog is being boss	When was the last time they went for a walk? Are they getting enough exercise? Your dog has learnt to pull because you have taught them that when they pull they get where they want to go.
Won't come when called	My dog thinks it's funny to run off	Have you told them off previously when they have come to you? Is your dog more interested in what's around them than they are in you? Do you have something to motivate them to return to you? How can you become more interesting and fun to them at times like this?
Barks at me when I have food	My dog is dominant	Has your dog ever been given attention when they have barked? Has your dog ever been given food when they bark? This is not dominance, this is a reflection of your leadership and relationship with your dog. You have inadvertently reinforced a behaviour you don't want and your dog has learnt how to get what they want through control.

Listen to your dog. In fact, listen to your child, your friend, your partner and your colleague. Take just a moment to see where they are coming from and it will help you to understand what questions to ask and what approach to take.

CAN MY CHILD AND DOG GET ALONG?

It is in a child's nature to be intrigued by the world and, for whatever reason, children are drawn in particular to dogs. Wherever I go with Chester, children will invariably declare to the world that there is a dog, or if they know him they will squeal his name, and sometimes even run towards him, regardless of whether he wants to say hello or not. That's the thing about kids. They have such an innocence and naivety to them, but at the same time, they are consumed completely by themselves and their own needs.

Young children, while sharing many similarities to dogs, including similar levels of cognition, emotion and size, are the most likely to be growled at, bitten and even killed by dogs in this world. According statistics provided by the Australian Veterinary Association, most dog bites affect children under fifteen years of age. Additionally, children are at least three times more likely to experience a bite needing medical attention than adults.

And as devastating as this is, to me it is no surprise. I cannot tell you the amount of times I have observed a child approach a dog without warning and attempted to corner the dog so they can touch them. If I hadn't been there in each instance to physically block a child or provide an escape for Chester, there is no doubt in my mind that he would have eventually growled, snapped at and possibly even bitten a child by now.

Being Chester's guardian, much like a parent is for their child, I am often put in a position where I am umpiring interactions between a dog and a child. I have received many judgmental looks by parents at cafes, where their child has approached Chester and I have stepped in between them to explain to the child that Chester has feelings too. I can imagine people look at his breed – Staffordshire bull terrier – then see my protective behaviours and immediately make the incorrect connection that I have a dangerous dog and that he might bite their child.

The truth is, I can never guarantee that he wouldn't. I could never guarantee any dog won't bite, regardless of breed. A dog goes through a series of progressive emotional stages before resorting to a bite:

1. Initial attention
2. Uncertainty
3. Insecurity
4. Fear
5. Attempt to escape or avoid
6. Inability to escape or avoid
7. The growl
8. The snap
9. The bite

Regardless of how subtle or overt, a dog will always attempt to communicate their emotional state to you and those around them.

Most often, I see dog owners and parents allow the dog to reach stage 6, when stage 1 was as far as anyone should have gone. With the correct precautions, dogs are not an inherent threat to a child at all. They have been domesticated over thousands (maybe even tens of thousands) of years to integrate into our families with eternal loyalty. They are a child's best teacher. They can teach children to see the world from a viewpoint that no parent can ever show. They can encourage them to explore, to use all their senses, to play and laugh like never before and to understand love outside of their own species. They can teach an appreciation for the natural world and their part within it.

Perhaps even more importantly, dogs can help teach children to be good people. They can teach them to consider others' feelings, to show respect, compassion, self-control, and to develop a sense for what is fair. We know from studies that animals do influence how children feel about the world, and in educational programs animals play an invaluable role in providing confidence, relaxation and general happiness to students. Having a dog in your family is exactly the same.

SUMMARY

Empathy is such an important trait. Whilst it is valuable to the cohesion of social bonds, it can also be exhausting. Learn how to apply cognitive empathy outside your family circle and preserve your emotions for those you love and care for. Learn to identify the feelings of your dog by stepping back and seeing things from his point of view. Get to understand his body language and behaviours so that you can set him up for success in this world. Most of our social connections are harnessed by seeing life through another's lens.

Did you know . . . *many people are increasingly leaving their dogs as beneficiaries in their will? Perhaps this was popularised by Countess Karlotta Liebenstein, who left more than one hundred million dollars to her Alsatian in 1992. It is reported that over one million Americans have left their dogs as primary beneficiaries.*

6.

Control and Predictability

Our brain is the centre of control for our body. It is where decisions are made, consciously or subconsciously, that ultimately determine if we survive each and every day. A lot of our actions are already involuntarily controlled by our brains; whether that be filling your lungs with air or pumping blood throughout your body. It is incredible how the brain just knows what to do. It contains 90 billion neurons (nerve cells) lined together by trillions of connectors (synapses), and it's thought that it would take 82 000 processors running on the world's fastest computer to imitate the brain for just one second. However, the brain does it much better and on just a few volts.

The remarkable evolution of the human brain got me to thinking about control. Even as I sit here right now, writing this book, much of my behaviour is driven by reflexes, not conscious thought. Much of what I am doing was decided upon hundreds of thousands of years ago. From how wonderfully conserving my brain is of precious energy, to the knowledge I receive of hunger as my stomach rumbles, we are running as a subconscious machine based on the best evolutionary adaptations to date.

YOUR MIND TRICKS YOU

Here's a fun experiment to demonstrate how control works in the mind. Find a set of coloured pencils or pens. Put them to your side, within reach but not where you can actually see them. Look straight ahead and randomly select a pencil without the knowledge of what colour it is.

Hold your arm out straight and to your side, in a ninety-degree angle to your head. While you look straight ahead, gradually move the pencil closer and closer to the front of your face until you can recognise what colour it is.

How close was it before you knew its colour? For most of us, the pencil needs to be very close to the front of our face before we can recognise its colour.

Try this again, but this time use the same coloured pencil and see if you need to move it as close to the front of your face before you can actually see the colour.

Did you find that you could actually see the colour of the pencil much quicker?

Because your brain already knew what colour it was, it tricked you into thinking you could actually see it earlier than what was visually possible for the human brain.

Everything in your periphery is essentially made up. Your brain has remembered your environment and constructed an illusion to help you make better sense of your surroundings. It helps you to feel in control.

Control then must be important for survival. It must help us to understand the world we live in and perhaps even exploit it. While my brain may unconsciously tell me I need food through the empty feeling in my stomach, actually finding the food requires a far more sophisticated adaptation. It requires planning, strategising and outsmarting, whether it be through hunting, foraging or scavenging. It requires a conscious effort and after hundreds of thousands of years successfully acquiring resources, our conscious brain has been reinforced into believing it has some form of control.

Let's turn our attention now to your mind. When I think about the mind, I see it as different to the brain. The mind is about our awareness, our thoughts and our emotions. It is where we make judgements and where we reason. It is ultimately responsible for how we perceive the world. Whether we see life as a dreary collection of depressing events or a beautiful privilege, is very much determined by our perception of it. How we see this world and our place within it all comes down to how well we can control our mind. This concept linking our sense of control to our general happiness can be applied to our dogs as well.

CASE STUDY

A Jack Russell terrier, remarkably called Jack, was introduced to me a while back. I adore Jack Russells! Whilst I generalise the breed, which goes against a lot of what I believe about dog behaviour, so many do seem to be an embodiment of several traits that I admire in dogs. Their inquisitive nature, tenacity, intelligence and, of course, excellent sense of humour, are characteristics among countless others that I adore.

As proof of why I'm hesitant to generalise breeds, Jack was not tenacious, nor was he inquisitive or curious. Instead, he hid under the dining-room table upon my arrival, with a look in his eye of absolute terror.

His owners, Jan and Trevor, treasured him. They had brought him home at just six weeks old (at least a week too early to be separated from his mother and siblings) and exposed him to a world of unconditional love. He was an inside dog (allowed regular access to indoors during the day and over night, as I believe all dogs should have), but despite the love they had shown him, he was experiencing some severe problems.

After I spent an entire hour chatting with his owners, Jack finally approached my irresistible hand, full of warm roast chicken that I had brought with me. He gently accepted the metaphorical handshake I offered and we got to know each other. Soon, Jack was back to being the happy dog that his owners said he was capable of being. He was delightful, wagging his tail and moving from one human to the next in an attempt to profit from displaying his innocent brown eyes. We laughed at how manipulative our beloved dogs are and Jan and Trevor tended to Jack by picking him up and holding him in the air like a baby. As I observed, Jack struggled, trying to weasel himself out of Jan's hands, bellowing out a growl I would have expected from a dog twice his size. After Jan gave him a few maternal and adoring lifts up in the air, she put him down and released him back to the floor.

We began talking about Jack and his problems and before Jan could finish describing his idiosyncratic quirks, I saw them with my own eyes. Jack trotted off to the lounge room, which could be seen from where we were sitting, and began engaging in a most bizarre series of behaviours. Firstly, he lay down and began licking his paws with an intensity that unnerved his owners. Jack then stopped, stood up and began to stare at the wall. He stood there in what appeared a catatonic state, like he had seen a ghost and nothing could distract him. But then a car approaching the end of the driveway broke his gaze and he moved on to the last part of the disturbing repertoire: the tail-chase. Not only had we all witnessed a strange series of events, he repeated the behaviours and became more and more intense as the son who had arrived in their driveway entered the house.

I sat there and watched the dynamics in this household. I knew there was a history here, and the family were omitting essential clues to the story they described of Jack's anxieties. But I didn't need to hear it from them. Jack was telling me everything I needed to know. Still, I sat there and said nothing.

Ryan, the son, approached Jack to engage in his home-arrival ritual. He picked Jack up and spun him around like parents do when pretending their child is an aeroplane. He was rough with Jack, but not cruel, and Jack struggled relentlessly until Ryan put him down. Jack ran over to the same position he was five minutes before and began to furiously lick his paws again. After my introduction to his cyclical, repetitive behaviours, I watched him with an expectation of each move and he didn't let me down. Each motion was eerily identical to the time before and once we watched his final chase around the tail-catching track, he began all over again.

I approached Jack, who mirrored my movements in appeasement, and I examined him. His front paws were bald and raw and the very end of his tail was scabbed as a painful reminder of the times in which his tail-chase was successful. I looked into his eyes and my heart sank. Here was an animal in a human world, with absolutely no control.

One of the topics I raise with dog owners is the issue of control. As humans, we impose a great deal of control over our entire social and working lives, but rarely do I see dog owners appreciate that the control they impose over their dog can have devastating effects.

I gave Jack the last of my roast chicken on his bed and left him in peace to eat it. As I sat back down on my chair, I felt a nudge against my right leg. Jack had come to me wanting more chicken. I smiled at him and let him smell my hands and once he discovered there was no more food, he calmly went back to his bed. Jan, Trevor and Ryan sat opposite me, staring, waiting for me to reach into my bag and deliver the magic pill that would fix all of Jack's problems.

I did reach into my bag, but instead of finding a pill or a wand, I pulled out a pad of paper and a pen and gently pushed it over to the other side of the table. I told them to write down what I was about to tell them in their own words. I told them that Jack was an emotional and sensitive dog. Because of this, he was easily aroused and could become stressed, particularly when he did not feel in control. I then asked them to write down what happens just before Jack begins the 'thing', as they described his odd behaviour. They all looked at each other and after some encouraging prompts from me, they finally saw the pattern. Every time Jack's sense of control was violated, he became anxious, moved away and began controlling his own mind and body in a series of repetitive behaviours. I told the family that to regain Jack's trust, that they must never violate him again, including picking him up, spinning him around and lifting him up in the air.

Using the CPR principles, I asked them to be *consistent* in their approach, *patient* as he begins to learn that he has control over his space again and *respectful* by seeing life through his beady little eyes instead of through theirs.

They heeded my advice and called me three months later, in celebration of Jack's successful transition. Jack had completely stopped the 'thing' because they were able to see where he was coming from. They showed empathy for their little mate and gave him the things in life he needed, including more exercise, time on his own without being disturbed and regular, fun training, where he learnt to control his resources by being cooperative with the humans around him.

DISPLACEMENT BEHAVIOURS

Dogs who displace their anxieties through unhelpful, repeated behaviours all yearn for a sense of control. Increasing their exercise helps, but mental exercise is just as beneficial. Keeping their brain active through positive and voluntary interactions such as play, obedience training and problem solving games helps to build confidence and purpose in a dog. During times when we have confidence and purpose, we feel most in control.

Displacement behaviours are any excessive or repetitive behaviours your dog displays, such as:

- Licking body parts, especially paws and legs
- Chasing tail
- Barking
- Howling
- Pacing
- Stiff body language
- Mounting other dogs

To overcome this, focus your dog on positive behaviours throughout the day that lead to a reward. Here are some examples of how to teach your dog to refocus:

- Cue your dog to sit
- Cue them to lie on their bed
- Engage in quick obedience sessions
- Teach them to focus on you
- Teach them to bring a ball back

- Teach them to walk beside you
- Play hide and seek or other mind and body games
- Engage in general exercise together
- Try problem solving tasks (using treat dispensers or toys)
- Play – with other dogs or people

If you are sitting down watching TV, choose a few of the examples from above and engage in some fun with your dog. If you play for two minutes each ad break over an hour-long TV show, you are spending fifteen minutes of positive time with your dog.

It's not just our dogs who exhibit displacement behaviours when they feel anxious or uncertain, someone who is uncomfortable in a social setting may express similar behaviours. Consider these common human displacement behaviours:

- Nervous laughter
- Touching face, body
- Crossing arms
- Pacing
- Excessive talking
- Hair touching
- Fiddling with hands
- Moving items around
- Avoiding eye contact

While we know that having complete control is ultimately an illusion, feeling some sense of control is clearly a part of our consciousness that we can't live successfully without. It's the same for our dogs.

From the time when our ancestors of the Upper Palaeolithic Period selected the wolf that was the most appeasing and cooperative animal to cohabit with them, the destiny of the domestic dog has been under our control. However, that doesn't mean they are always okay with it. Which is why it is vital to provide a cooperative relationship in which we empower our dogs to work under having the illusion of control.

Through encouraging positive ways to control resources, such as reinforcing the 3 Cs – *calm*, *cooperative* and *controlled* behaviours – you can make your dog think they have control. By doing so, your dog's sense of self-worth skyrockets and they learn pro-social ways to engage with their owners, other dogs and themselves.

Under the positive illusion of control, and with consistent, patient and respectful interactions, displacement behaviours will reduce and even come to an end.

Without a sense of control, your dog is susceptible to engaging in counterproductive and distressing behaviours, like we saw in Jack, or much worse.

THE DOMINANCE MYTH

Control is also frequently linked to the concept of dominance in canid packs. If you watch a pack of wolves in an enclosure, you will see a range of interesting dynamics, some that you may even see in a pack of domestic dogs. You may see play, you may see fights over resources such as food or over mates, and you might even see smaller groups form within the enclosed population to create more than one pack, both competing for the resources they had once attained through cooperation.

We have used this observation of captive wolf populations as parallels to our understanding of the modern dog, but there were two fallacies we ignored. Firstly, our dogs are not wolves and, secondly, these wolves are not wild.

They are captive. Observing captive populations rarely provides us with a comparison for wild behaviour. If we wanted to base our understanding of the modern dog on true wolf behaviour, then we needed to observe wolves in the wild.

And eventually we did, but not until the late 1990s. Observers of wild canids discovered that, certainly, they live in groups, but that the structure or 'hierarchy' was remarkably different to what we had seen in captive populations. The hierarchy in the wild was fluid and often interchangeable between individuals. It consisted of a family, instead of a group of unrelated individuals as it may have in captivity, usually with both parents and juvenile offspring. Dominance was a behaviour that existed to maintain the bond between individuals; it was a behaviour we might prefer to describe as leadership. It was observed that parents were inherent leaders and that cooperation of the family was essential for survival. When young wolves grew into adulthood, they would naturally disperse and create their own family to live out their rest of their lives with. In captivity, this rarely happens.

So if dogs are not naturally dominant creatures, why then do we see behaviours that make us feel they are? Remember Jack who displaced his anxieties about having no control by licking, chasing his tail and staring? Well, some dogs learn other ways of gaining control over things they need and want and, again, we inadvertently reinforce it. And while these perceivably 'dominant' behaviours may be antagonising, bossy and sometimes even dangerous, we only have ourselves to blame.

So how does your dog indicate they are trying to control your behaviours? Below are some behaviours you may notice your dog doing, which may have previously been put down to having a 'dominant' dog:

- Blocking your movements
- Pushing into you for a response – don't confuse this with a dog leaning against you, which is not a controlling behaviour
- Pulling on lead
- Lunging, growling or biting at people or other animals
- Barking at you

Please note that any behaviour that endangers your dog, other animals or people should be managed with the support of a qualified and experienced behaviourist and/or veterinarian.

VIOLENCE BETWEEN DOGS IN THE HOME

Sometimes dogs will attempt to exert control over other dogs. I cannot begin to tell you how common dog-on-dog fighting is in households. Two dogs who have grown up together in absolute harmony all of a sudden want to kill each other over a stick that was being thrown in the backyard.

While we know our dogs are not wolves, the wolf is still our dogs' common ancestor. The wolf is the living fossil and the basis for how we have come to understand their domestic counterpart. In families, wolves will raise their pups to be strong and manipulative dogs. The young will learn how to hunt, to find a mate, to migrate for water and to avoid danger. In the wild, a dog has true purpose.

Once that wolf pup reaches adulthood, they leave the pack. But when a pup reaches adulthood in the domestic setting, they stay and live out their days with the same family they started with. They are never able to disperse and find their own family, but instead are expected to exist without frustration in a family they naturally may not be attracted to. This is often where we encounter problems.

As two dogs reach adulthood (at around two years of age, give or take a year or two) they instinctively yearn to form their own group. Sometimes one or more dogs in a family setting turn on another – who becomes the social outcast – as they make an ill-fated attempt to form their own 'family'. Unfortunately, no matter what you do to prevent this from happening, it still can occur and can be very difficult to curb.

If this has happened in your family, it is important to accept that you may never be able to integrate the group back into harmony, as relationships may have already been too damaged. But there are things you can do to try to rebuild relationships based on mutual trust and respect.

Firstly, if your dogs can be together, it is important that they are not permitted to attempt any controlling behaviours over you. Usually, the fighting is elicited by an owner's interaction with one dog over the other, so it is imperative that any interaction with your dogs is a pro-social behaviour – the best types involve exercise and cooperation.

Your dogs are desperate for your positive guidance. Engaging in activities that require strong group cooperation is essential. In other words, all your dogs need to work together to get what they want.

Strategies for improving the relationship between two or more dogs include:

- Allow them to exhaust physically. Pent up energy can result in frustrated and redirected behaviours.
- Keep their minds engaged in positive activities
- Make cooperating with each other essential to getting what they want
- Engage in obedience classes

- Provide consistent leadership and mean what you say and do
- Be patient with them when guiding them into pro-social behaviours
- Respect where they are coming from. See their point of view and make decisions based on what is best for them.
- Feed them separately and only when they are calm, cooperative and controlled (the 3 Cs)
- Find a qualified and trusted behaviourist to help you implement helpful strategies

Try as you might however, sometimes a dog cannot integrate back into the family and may become permanently ostracised. If this happens, you need to make a decision on what is best for the dog. Sometimes, as heartbreaking as it may be, your dog deserves to feel a part of a loving family and that family may not be yours. If this does happen, get in contact with the appropriate breed club for advice on rehoming the dog in question. Advertising a dog online, particularly 'free to a good home', runs the risk of them falling into the wrong hands.

PREDICTABILITY AND ANXIETY

Are you ticklish? I am! Just a look from someone with that tickling-monster glimmer in their eye makes my adrenal glands burst with the flight response as I run and giggle away from the potential offender. But what if you tickle yourself? Why doesn't it work?

It doesn't work because we already know it's going to happen. The cerebellum, which is located at the base of the brain and plays a major role in muscle reflexes and responses, already predicts the sensation of a tickle and so instead of alerting the other parts of the brain to respond, it cancels them, in a sort of 'don't worry, we already know what happens here' communication across its wirings.

While some of us may like to think of ourselves as adventure-seeking adrenaline junkies, the truth is we are very much creatures of habit. Even adventure sports like sky diving have a fair element of predictability to them. Being able to predict outcomes to events helps us manage stress. It helps us to decide on the best action to take and it helps us make sense of things that otherwise appear abstract.

Historically, being able to predict the environment may very well have meant the difference between being devoured by a sabre-toothed tiger and narrowly escaping its clutches. It is so hardwired into our brain because it is undoubtedly one of the pillars of success and survival for all living species.

So what happens when we *can't* control or predict our environment? This matrix below shows some of the feelings we may experience.

	Predictable	**Unpredictable**
Controllable	Optimism	Anxiety
Uncontrollable	Frustration	Learned helplessness

Looking at the table, you can see how our perception of our environment and our place within it can greatly affect how we feel and behave. Namely:

- When we feel in control and are able to predict our environment, we feel a sense of optimism

- When we feel somewhat in control of our environment, but cannot predict it, we feel anxious
- When we are able to predict the environment, but have no sense of control over it, we become frustrated
- When we can neither predict nor control our environment, we eventually surrender to a learned helplessness

We may see learned helplessness in a dog that has been outcast and attacked by other dogs in its family, as described earlier. One of the most common causes of behavioural issues in dogs is anxiety. Learned helplessness is chronic anxiety with no end in sight.

Anxiety is a common source of distress in humans too. Those who suffer from anxiety are generally hypervigilant and on constant lookout for the unexpected. The more we feel we can predict our environment, the more we believe we are in control. But at the same time, anxiety has a power so strong that it can make you feel a range of emotional and physical symptoms all at the same time and often without warning. It is that voice within you that fills you with self-doubt and uncertainty, making you question everything and everyone. But whilst many may feel the relentless talons of anxiety dig into their shoulders and chest, it doesn't mean that it can't be managed, even wrangled a little and defeated. Interestingly, the more we help our dogs overcome anxiety, the more we help ourselves.

Our dogs are complete, comprehensive creatures of habit. Each day on your walk, your dog is predicting that German short-haired pointer who routinely gallops up and down his fence with indiscriminate contempt. They predict the particular sound of scrunched plastic packaging that results in a treat. Your dog even predicts what your shoes mean. Your work shoes, your walking shoes, your heels. They all mean something very different to your dog and to them it is information essential to their survival.

While we appreciate that these furry critters may only flourish in environments that are certain and pleasant, unfortunately the world in which we coexist doesn't always permit this. Unforseen storms can impose themselves on a tree nearby, garbage trucks can approach us from around the corner and people can behave in ways that leave dogs confused about their relationships, causing a breakdown of their sense of security that was strong only moments ago. Reality bites!

So how can you create a predictable environment for your dog, in which they feel safe, in control and stimulated all at the same time? Well, it's all about changing how your dog perceives the world, changing their associations and empowering them to predict their environment positively. Here are some practical steps you can take to achieve this:

- Create a safe place for your dog inside: a place that is warm and quiet, and near you at times in which you are the most calm and content
- In times of uncertainty, remove your dog from the stimulus. There are some things that you can't control, but what you can manage is your response, so a swift and fun U-turn is often very helpful if you are outside with them.
- Change your dog's association from something they are anxious about to something positive. For example, if your dog is nervous around other dogs, reward them for looking at another dog then increase the distance between them, making your dog feel safe and positive about the experience.

Often putting the focus of the other dog on cue is helpful too. Just like Emma and her border collie Jet, pair the association of yummy food with encouraging words like 'Let's play!' or 'There's a dog!' Help your dog learn that other dogs are not a threat, rather they are an opportunity for a reward. Once your dog understands that 'There's a dog!' means yummy food and safety, you can apply this strategy out on your walks when you see a dog. You can apply this to anything your dog is uncertain of or reactive to.

Make sure however that you are always in a position to control the environment and are setting your dog up for success. Anxious dogs are motivated by safety. Make sure you are able to make your dog feel safe, even if that is with a quick U-turn in the opposite direction.

There is no doubt that control and predictability are ingrained into our conscious and subconscious. And while we acknowledge that life is full of uncertainties, we are still here, alive and in existence with our dogs. So as long as that great star in the sky continues to burn and as long as we are here together, we owe it to both ourselves and our dogs to make the very best of what we have.

SUMMARY

Whilst control and predictability are unattainable in the grand scheme of things, our subconscious still needs to believe they are achievable. Always try to give your dog a sense of positive control and predictability. Identify your dog's emotional state by observing their behaviour and look out for anxiety and frustration. Set up situations in which they can feel in control of their resources, as well as their safety, by cooperating with you. It is imperative that as their leader you are observant and always in a position to set your dog up for success.

Did you know . . . *dogs will urinate on objects that stick up, such as trees and poles? The taller the better. It has been reported that dogs urinating on poles is so common in Croatia that many street poles have decayed and collapsed because of the acidic chemicals in dogs' urine!*

7.
Seize the Good Moments

'Sit, sit, sit, sit, sit, sit, sit, sit, sit, sit. SIT. No! NO! Sit. GOOD boy.'

The dog sits.

What has just happened? In what may sound to the dog like the incessant melody of a novice tenor, the command to sit was actually nothing more than a confused and frustrated query. Why is that? If I may, I'd like to let you in on a little secret. This dog has known how to sit well before he and his owner had even met.

When a dog is born, he arrives with little skill. He is deaf and blind, unable to maintain his body temperature or urinate and defecate without the assistance of his mother. He instinctively gravitates to his siblings for warmth, attempting by trial and error to reach a feeding spot in between them, and with each nutritious suckle of his mother's milk, he grows. His seemingly futile attempts to support his body weight serve to build muscle strength and as he side-winds along the floor his ability to explore and develop within the world is enhanced.

By day fourteen, his days of rigorous strength-building mean he can now stand with an unsteady waver until he falls down and attempts to stand up again. His ears begin to clear and soon he will be able to absorb the sounds and sights of his littermates and mother. You may hear him rehearse his newfound vocal cords and notice that he is developing quickly, taking the small form of the dog he will one day be.

By day twenty-one, his sensory and motoric organs become acquainted, which is evident in his attempts to interact with his brothers and sisters, and the purposeful tail wag he expresses his emotions through. His body is warmed without others to support it, his razor-sharp teeth begin to erupt and he is able to eliminate waste independently.

Between day twenty-eight and his eighth week of life, the puppy embarks on social development that arguably determines much of who he becomes and how he feels throughout his life. His owners prepare him for the future and encourage him to explore his environment, introducing him to the benign and the dangerous, hoping he successfully understands the difference. He experiments with his motor skills through infantile play: running, rolling and dropping through the long grass as he spiritedly stalks his sisters ahead. At this stage, he is prepared for his new and hopefully forever home, where he has already mastered much of what his new owner will attempt to teach him.

Have a look at your dog right now. What are they doing? Wherever they are, I imagine they are calm. Stand up, go to the biscuit tin and give them a reward. Go on! I'll wait for you.

You have just seized a moment of tranquillity in your dog; a moment you want to encourage and reinforce. As a dog's 'trainer' we accept far more credit than we deserve. Puppies can sit, drop, roll, speak, stand, heel, and fetch well before we thrust upon them our expectations and impositions. We are not imparting any new knowledge of the basics and certainly not anything they hadn't already discovered by trial and error themselves.

We are not really their trainers: we are their colleagues. We celebrate achievements together, encourage good choices with them and support them during times of uncertainty and distress. We don't tell them what to do, but we empower them to initiate positive and collaborative choices. We teach them not to do, but to think.

Successful collegial relationships involve teamwork, alliance, collaboration and companionship. While there is an inherent hierarchy in your relationship with your dog, much of it is based on leadership.

LEADERSHIP

The American author John Maxwell once said: 'Leaders become great not because of their power, but their ability to empower others.' I think there's a lot in that.

Leadership is quite a subjective trait. Some see it as the ability to lead a group and nothing more, while others see it as a gift to create great change. As your dog's leader, you have the power to be anything. As dogs have evolved with us, it is clear they are our followers. How good you are as their leader then is determined more by whether they follow you by choice, or whether they follow you by force.

I often use the term 'capturing' when I'm helping clients. It's almost like taking a snapshot of the behaviour you want and rewarding it as it happens. Capturing a behaviour can only occur when it is happening on its own. You can't capture something if you have requested it or enforced it. The dog hasn't made their own choice.

Capturing good choices in our dogs is an example of great leadership. When you capture a behaviour, the dog is not forced by you to behave in a certain way, but rather empowered to make a good decision on their own. Most of my dog Chester's behaviours are his own choice. He has learnt through my patient and persistent leadership that he can acquire most of what he wants in life by controlling his own behaviour.

In times when he is calm, I am consistently there to capture that very moment he is in. In times of cooperation, I immediately acknowledge his initiative and reward him with something he wants. In times of self-control, I am at his side to celebrate incredible acts of cognitive forethought. I have been there at his side every time he has instigated a choice that is conducive to a safe, happy and healthy existence, never once telling him how.

But what are we capturing exactly? You should acknowledge and reinforce the choices a dog makes that builds their confidence and a bond between you both.

REMEMBER THE 3 CS

- Calm
- Cooperative
- Controlled

We want to encourage these within our dogs as much as we possibly can. Let's look at each one in more detail.

The calm

With dogs generally resting over fourteen hours a day, capturing the calm seems very achievable. Outside of rest, however, our dogs are exposed to a world that they have little control over. Some ten hours a day are made up of countless little moments where your dog is aware and alert. They are observing, exploring and reacting to their ever-changing environment and at every moment they are making choices. If you watch your dog closely during these waking hours, you will be able to see what they are thinking by their response to the world.

When are they most calm? Identify these moments and set them up to occur more often. If your dog is very nervous and has trouble being calm – around other dogs at a park, for instance – observe what they are doing in these moments. I would expect to see signs of uncertainty, including body shakes and a yawn. Their tail would stiffen, be placed in-between their legs, and each ear movement or head turn would express anxiety and hypervigilance. This environment is not conducive to the calm state of mind you are trying to capture. So what should you do? Walk your dog back to the side of the park where it is quiet and where they feel safe. Your dog will feel calm and in this moment you will be there to reward it.

The more your dog feels safe in your hands, the more confident they become. Creating environments where your dog feels calm builds trust and, when applied consistently, your dog gradually desensitises from what once was a real threat to a benign part of existing in a human world. Examples of calm dog behaviours include:

- Having a relaxed tail
- Having ears softly folded back
- Having a soft mouth and relaxed body

- Being responsive to you
- Being quiet and content
- Resting on a bed
- Not being distracted by their environment
- Happily being out of your sight
- Willingly exploring their environment with a loose and relaxed lead
- Gladly taking food from you

Look out for these behaviours and encourage them as much as possible.

The cooperative

A process of working together to reach the same end is how many define cooperation. The wild dogs who moved closer to our ancestors' camps, followed them on hunts and kept them warm during blistering winters were the most cooperative dogs. Cooperation was what brought two unlikely species together to coexist many thousands of years ago.

Dogs instinctively want to cooperate with us. It is in their DNA for survival and a characteristic that we can harness to not only improve their behaviour, but to also improve our relationship with them.

So how do we identify cooperation? Every time your dog shows signs of working with you, they are cooperating. When they look at you on a walk, when they follow you at the park, when they chase the ball and return it, they are cooperating. Your dog is collaborating with you all the time. They are putting up their end of the bargain each and every day, but are you there to reciprocate it? Examples of dogs cooperating include:

- Focusing on you in unfamiliar environments
- Following your gaze or hand signals

- Moving back towards you when uncertain of a stimulus
- Following you in unfamiliar environments
- Playing with you

With every cooperative act your dog volunteers, they are expressing their feelings about their relationship with you. They are showing you that they trust and respect you.

Play is an excellent example of how we can develop a cooperative relationship with our dogs. One of Chester's favourite activities is to fetch a stick from the water. But once he finds the stick, how does it make itself back into the water for him to retrieve again? I, of course, am there to provide this part of the cooperative bargain. I throw the stick into the water, just deep enough so that Chester is comfortable rescuing it, and he returns it back to me and gently drops it in my hand. He then bounds back into the ankle-deep water in the direction he predicts it will need to be rescued from again. Together we exist in that moment, capturing each other's positive play behaviours and cooperating to reach the same goal.

Think now of what your dog loves to do. Find out what it is and become involved. Cooperate with them so that they can benefit from the positivity of your involvement. Watch them begin to see you as an integral player in the activity and help them understand how working with you makes the activity so much more meaningful. They will see you not just as a leader but also as a loyal comrade who they share a strong bond with. Examples of cooperative play include:

- Tug of war – sometimes you win, other times they win
- Fetching and retrieving the ball

- Scattering food to find in the backyard
- Hiding a toy and searching for it
- Guessing which cup the treat is under
- Chasing each other
- Agility games
- Heel and release games

The controlled

Controlling the desire for immediate gratification is arguably the most difficult behaviour in humans. In fact, of the many disorders millions of people are diagnosed with each year, impulse control disorders such as obsessive compulsion, pathological gambling and avoidance are among the most debilitating.

The prefrontal cortex of the brain is where we make cognitive decisions, assess risks and plan; our rational brain. This part of the frontal lobe remains underdeveloped until we are well into our adulthood. While this matter makes up 30 per cent of the brain in humans, for dogs, it's roughly 13 per cent. We can clearly see we have an advantage over them when it comes to making rational decisions.

As the colleague and guardian of our dogs, we are responsible for planning the future, foreseeing dangers and applying logic when making decisions. The difference between us setting up impulse control in our dogs' choices and not doing so can be the difference between your dog sitting at the curb or running across the road and being hit by a car. It can literally be a choice of life or death. While a dog may not understand how to plan for the future, they do understand immediate risks and rewards, so there is no reason we can't capture small moments of self-control and build from them.

An important part of capturing self-control in your dog is

doing so *before* they act impulsively. If Chester sees a rabbit in the distance, I reward him for looking at the rabbit but staying with me. In this particular moment, his choice to look back at me should be reinforced with something that is similar to his motivation for chasing the rabbit. A good honest predator/prey tug-of-war game played together works perfectly.

I know he is thinking about the rabbit. He is assessing the value versus effort of chasing it and I am in a strong position to empower him to make a choice based on impulse control. By simply acknowledging him looking, I am reinforcing him considering his options and making a decision to come to me for a reward instead of the rabbit. I have reinforced a good choice that he has made all on his own and next time he sees a rabbit, he is far more likely to look to it, then look to me.

Capturing impulse control can be applied at every moment your dog is thinking about a behaviour or response before actually making a decision. Examples of your dog exercising self-control include:

- Volunteering to sit for a reward
- Choosing to go to their bed without being asked
- Waiting patiently for something they want
- Not jumping up
- Not barking for something they want
- Choosing not to chase another animal and to come to you instead
- Moving away when unsure of a stimulus
- Coming to you in times of uncertainty
- Being quiet (not barking/whining)
- Being gentle at times when they are excited

Notice that none of these behaviours have been asked of the dog, the dog is choosing to offer them instead.

WHY IS IT SO HARD TO CAPTURE THE GOOD?

Capturing the good moments seems to be so difficult for humans to do. Each and every day of our lives something good happens, but our nature is to gravitate to what is negative. It comes from our need to control our environment. When something good is happening, there is no threat to survival. In today's society, however, it is so important to acknowledge the good moments and relish them, no matter how simple they are.

Understandably, nobody ever contacts me to tell me about the good in their dog. They don't see this as my job. Unfortunately, this is part of the problem. Your dog will do something great at least fifty times a day, but odds are you are missing most of it.

Every day I take my dogs for a walk and we encounter a series of potential threats that would leave any reactive dog exhausted with stress and anxiety. Adjacent to my home there are two magnificent maremmas, originally bred for their prowess in protecting sheep in the Abruzzo and Maremma regions of central Italy. With this protective instinct, bred over thousands of years, these two dogs enthusiastically guard their property as we walk past. They start before we even step on to the road, furiously pacing up and down the fence.

One of the best things I have captured with Chester is his exquisite impulse control and trust in me as his protector. While the maremmas are guardians of their land, I am the guardian of my dog. I watch Chester walk beside me (off his lead) down the road and feel the crescendo of frustration in the maremmas as we approach. Chester trots ahead of me and I say nothing. He looks over to them and his tail stiffens along with his body. Then, he licks his lips.

(Remember lip licking is usually for one of two reasons: to enhance the olfactory senses or to express anxiety and uncertainty.)

I don't say anything to him, because I know what he is thinking. I know that at this moment, I have a spectacular opportunity to capture impulse control at its best! Chester turns to look back and me and I smile. He runs back to me and at that moment I praise him excessively. What a wonderful decision he just made, all on his own! What confidence that builds within him and in our relationship together!

There will be moments each day when you and your dog have an opportunity like this. It may simply be that your dog walks up to the back door and doesn't jump on it, it may be that your dog goes to his bed instead of begging at the table, or it may be a moment that trumps these, where your dog sees a cat but looks immediately to you for a reward. How much these moments occur is directly related to how aware you are of your dog's thoughts and behaviours and how prepared you are to reinforce the good ones.

As I have already said, your dog will do something great at least fifty times a day. How often are you acknowledging and rewarding these things? How often are you empowering your dog? Let's answer this together. Find a piece of paper and pen and create a list of all the good things your dog does without being asked. It might look a little something like this:

- Sits for a treat
- Sits to get on the couch
- Stands patiently outside to come inside
- Waits patiently for his dinner

- Looks to me if unsure
- Goes to bed when tired
- Moves away from dogs who are reactive
- Lets others take food from where they are eating
- Walks beside me
- Waits to be asked onto the bed
- Remains calm in the car
- Sees a rabbit and looks away
- Sees a cat and runs back to me
- Stands at the door to go outside to the toilet
- Barks twice at a visitor and then runs to me

Think of similar behaviours in your dog and write them down. As you get to know your dog, the list will become longer and longer. What is most important is that you are identifying all the good stuff.

To me, as a 'canine behaviourist', these are the things that are most important in a companion dog. Whether my dog drops on a recall, heels perfectly on a right-about-turn or reliably fetches a rubber dumbbell from ten metres away is not important to me. Have I trained him to do all of these things? Yes, of course, but at the end of the day how well a dog behaves on command is not necessarily a reflection of how well they feel inside. I have met some dogs who are champions in competitive obedience trials, but the moment they get near another dog they are in a completely different state of mind and ready to attack. This is because some have specific times in their lives where they are required to behave well (usually for a single hour on the weekend during a trial) and times when they have no direction at all (usually the rest of the week!). Well behaved dogs do not necessarily have a positive state of mind.

Learning can occur in every interaction we have with our dogs. I would much rather see people incorporate the capturing strategies we've looked at in this chapter into their daily training routine than to focus on arbitrarily designed obedience rules that mean very little to their dog. This does not mean that obedience classes and trials are not a great exercise. I think any opportunity to spend time with your dog and your family is important, particularly opportunities to socialise in a positive environment. If you are serious about obedience trials, dock jumping or fly ball and your dog enjoys it, then I think that is wonderful. I encourage those who have not tried these sports to take their dog, watch and perhaps even participate, dog willing. However, it's vital to underpin such activities with proper guidance and leadership for your dog each and every day. Remember a happy dog is well behaved because they *want* to be, not because they *have* to be.

CAPTURING THE GOOD IN THOSE AROUND US

Good behaviours occur with people in our lives every day. Your partner might empty the dishwasher or your son might pick up his toy and put it away. However, humans and most social animals understandably focus on what needs to be controlled more than what is already being controlled. This is a survival adaptation to ensure that those in your family network are protected and safe from danger.

Within the realms of a modern and civilised world, however, the role of these natural instincts has changed. We now tend to focus on the need to control others to get what we *want* from them, instead of getting what we *need* to survive.

Interestingly, the more we try to enforce control on our

partners and our children, the more opposition we tend to receive from them. We can inadvertently develop a relationship that is not based on mutual trust and respect, but rather on fear, avoidance and resentment.

Ironically, it takes more time and energy to be negative than it does to be positive. Moreover, a negative disposition can have dire affects on your physiology, with correlations between negativity and heart disease being elucidated in countless research papers.

But how can you just switch from focusing on the negative to the positive? Can you really change who you are? Despite your brain working tirelessly to remind you there is looming danger in this world, you can actually defy its negativity bias and change the way you think. Challenging our brain activates various neural circuits, increasing the efficiency of how it communicates to the mind and body and helping it to solidify a new and more productive way of thinking.

The more we challenge the brain, the less energy it takes to change over time. This plasticity in our brain cells enables the new thought processes to be automatic. In other words, purposefully and consistently practising positivity can cause this process to become subconscious so that you no longer need to actively think to be positive – it just happens.

Let's do an exercise to consider this further. Grab a pen and a piece of paper and draw three columns. In the first column, write a list of the important people in your life (and your dog!). In the second column, write down the things you ask them to do on a daily basis without success. In the third column, write down how it would look if you didn't ask them to do something and they offered to do it instead. Here is an example:

PERSON/DOG	REQUESTS	VOLUNTARY ACTION
A staff member	Ask them to work harder	Staff member shows initiative to be friendly to a customer
Child	Ask them to put toys away	Child tidies room without being asked
Dog	Yell at your dog to stop barking at neighbours	Dog is quiet when neighbours arrive home

You can't get exactly what you want straight away. Capturing requires reinforcing bits at a time, until you build up the behaviour to what you want. This is called shaping.

Example

To get your child to tidy up their room without being asked, you would need to capture a series of little behaviours, such as rewarding them for putting a dirty sock in the laundry basket. You might initially need to ensure the laundry basket is within convenient reach. Then you may see them do it again, to which you will reward them with something they want again.

A little encouragement may be required to start it off, but when your child realises that offering these behaviours results in a combination of intrinsic and extrinsic rewards, they are more and more likely to offer you more the next time.

Whenever somebody does something voluntarily, that's your chance to acknowledge and encourage the behaviour. Just as we've seen with our dogs earlier in the chapter, this will help others in your life to think proactively and learn how to get what they want through their own volition.

There are many simple ways you can reinforce positive behaviours. If your colleague offers to cover a shift for you, you can show thanks by buying them a bunch of flowers. If your daughter starts her homework without being asked, you can acknowledge her effort and offer to help. If your dog waits quietly at the door to come inside, you can reward them by letting them in.

In these examples, we haven't asked any of them to do these behaviours, they have volunteered them and we have captured that moment with a reward. Of course, there are limits to what can be achieved in a short amount of time with such an approach, but the more we reinforce the positive choices of those around us, the more likely they are to continue making them. From a seemingly infinitesimal progression to a great leap towards the ultimate goal, each and every step should be acknowledged and celebrated.

An American psychology professor and dog expert named Stanley Coren wrote an article about the art of capturing the good moments, which he referred to as 'auto training', describing it as a method where the dog is actually teaching himself and you are just there to celebrate it with a reward. What is so wonderful about this approach is that it is fun! It reminds me of the educational adage that 'laughing kids learn' – the same goes for our dogs.

When you make a task fun, training through play not only becomes motivating, but research shows that the endorphins in our brain as well as our dog's brain are increased. Endorphins are found in the central nervous system and pituitary gland of humans and dogs, and are one of many neurotransmitters that interact with receptors in the brain to make us feel good.

Capturing behaviours can be applied with dogs of all ages, but I especially love seeing it used with puppies. Puppies are so new to this world and have an unquenchable thirst for learning, much like a toddler. They are constantly exploring with their eyes, ears and nose, not to mention their teeth and paws. They are such inquisitive little creatures and at this time in their lives they are eager to learn how to successfully exist in this world.

Much of what they learn comes from us, so it is incredibly important we do our best to get it right. We want to empower them, encourage them and build confidence within them. We want a dog to grow up into a calm, assured and content animal and the best way to do this is by letting them learn as much as they can themselves.

SUMMARY

Empowering others to think for themselves is crucial when it comes to building confidence and positive relationships. Instead of telling your dog what to do, sit back and observe what they are already doing. Any time they are voluntarily displaying calm, cooperative or controlled behaviours, capture the moment and reinforce it. Whilst you don't want to give your dog the freedom to make choices that are unsafe, you can set up scenarios in which your dog feels they are in control and making good choices. The more you empower your dog, the better behaved they are, and most importantly, the happier they are.

Did you know . . . *the most common command across the world is 'sit'? In French it is 'assis', in German it is 'sitz', in Spanish 'siéntate' and in Italian it is 'seduto'. No matter where a dog is from, they all speak the same language. The universality of their language makes me wonder if dogs are better linguists than we are.*

8.

Is It Puppy Love? Or Just Science?

Love is a raw, uncontrollable emotion we all yearn for. Despite the millions of years our brains have had to evolve to think, rationalise and plan, when it comes to love, the organ between our ears seems to resign itself to a senseless mush, completely vulnerable and disorientated.

I bet you feel this kind of mushy love for your dog. Is it a maternal/paternal love? A love based on friendship? A combination of the two? Whatever the answer, the love we have for a dog is love in its purest form. For many, it is a selfless love.

When we experience love our brain is in fact very active. When we feel passionate love a series of hormones are activated, causing our palms to perspire, our blood pressure to rise and our minds to feel euphoric. These hormones include adrenaline, dopamine, endorphins and oxytocin. But is it just love that makes us feel so good?

The simple acts of moving our bodies during exercise or laughing make us feel good by increasing endorphins in the brain. When your dog is active and having fun it improves their lives too! Playtime with our dogs goes beyond a simple physical engagement – it builds a very special bond.

Research tells us that when we stare into the eyes of our beloved dog, this also triggers a response in the brain that makes us both feel happy. However, when I first began learning about dog training, experienced experts would always say, 'Never stare into the eyes of a dog.' It was always described as a threatening behaviour, because in the wild animals believe that another animal staring at them is preying on them or is perhaps a dangerous competitor.

It makes sense, doesn't it? Wild predators have stereoscopic vision, meaning their eyes are positioned in front of their head to focus on the hunt. Prey animals such as herbivores like deer have panoramic vision, in which their eyes are positioned on the side of their head. In theory, this enables them to see a wider scope of their environment, to keep a constant lookout for predators.

Humans, like dogs, have stereoscopic vision. A common ancestor of man and monkey, Australopithecus afarensis (extant some three million years ago), commonly fell prey to large predators such as lions and leopards. So while we may not have evolved from predators, there must be an evolutionary advantage to having eyes at the front of our face.

Research suggests that having diverged from monkeys, who primarily seek refuge in trees, having stereoscopic vision is a clear survival advantage as it assists in the visual focus for which branch is ahead. A tree-dwelling animal with eyes on the side of its face wouldn't last long in a tree and no doubt those that tried, died out.

Nowadays the trees we spend most of our time in are during those precious moments of our childhood – our time seeking refuge in the natural world's treetops for anything more than fun seems to be a vision of the past. This got me to thinking about the other advantages the position of our eyes may have, particularly with regard to our social lives.

I spent a long time believing that making eye contact with a dog could be dangerous. And it can! Making eye contact with an unknown dog, particularly one who does not feel a sense of control in that moment, can make them feel anxious, resulting in avoidance or, worse, a bite. This can include dogs who are tied up or who are cornered by an innocent but antagonistic child pushing the limits for a pat.

But what about a dog who you love and share a bond with? Research tells us that eye contact with a dog we know may be of mutual benefit. The gaze can have the same mental and physical effects as when two emotionally involved people gaze at each other. Research in Japan found that dogs and their owners sharing a mutual gaze had higher levels of oxytocin, a neurochemical also known as the 'cuddle hormone' because it is released when people snuggle up together. To me, it's just another example of how strong the relationship between man and dog is.

A puppy in their vulnerability and naivety may look into your eyes with initial curiosity, wondering who you are and what you want. They may then engage in a stare with you so deep that time is halted and you are left realising that they need you more than you even realised. Your stare back is just as powerful and it has the ability to reveal to them your character, your intentions and your soul. If your puppy sees all this in you, they will know who you are, what you want and that you are the one they will grow to trust and respect.

SOCIALISING YOUR PUPPY

While the initial gaze between you and your puppy may be one of the first social transactions you have together, your actions are what cement the relationship. How you behave around them and how you prepare them for this world ultimately determines their triumphs and shortcomings. So you can either set them up to succeed or you can set them up to fail. Which one will you choose?

The principles of setting others up for success applies to those you lead, including your dogs and children. Ideally, we want to create a learning environment where they are safe and where you remain in control even when they encounter a distraction. In other words, you want to give them the illusion of choice and control when really it is you who oversees the learning process, as outlined in Chapter 6.

I love to train puppies off-lead as much as possible. There is something so impersonal and untrusting about training a puppy on-lead, particularly at a time in which you are trying to create a bond. However, if you are going to train your puppy off-lead then once again you must set them up to succeed.

It would be foolish to release a four-month-old puppy into the middle of an off-lead dog park for their first social encounter. Similarly, it would be just as naive to leave a child at their first day of primary school without exercising their social muscles long before that significant day. Children and dogs require a nurturing introduction to the world. We want their first impressions to be filled with hope and positivity. But achieving this for dogs and children requires quite different teachings.

Our children are raised in a way that prepares them for adulthood and independence. As they grow, they learn and they change. We raise them to become contributing members of society, to find their voice and to discover where they belong.

While dogs also reach adulthood, in a sense they never truly grow up. They are trapped in the confinement of domesticity, in which they are dependent on us across their entire life. While we may train resilience in our children – exposing them to small amounts of hardship and hurt in the hope they will learn to tolerate the inescapable sting of reality later in life – for our dogs, it is very different. Exposing our dogs completely to the world sets them up for a life of anxiety, fear and, ultimately, failure.

A child who is raised with a parent behind him every step of the way will remain a child forever. However, a dog who is raised without an owner behind her will grow into an adult but maintain the mind of a failed puppy.

CASE STUDY

His name was Bear, a tubby little staffy. A quintessential bull terrier filled with overt and tireless love and affection for all people. I met him at just eight weeks of age. His wide and hopeful eyes filled a head that rested trustingly in my hand and looked up at me, exposing a complete and honest vulnerability.

Bear was new to this old world. He hadn't met many outside his pack and so my novel presence overwhelmed him with an innocent enthusiasm so powerful the ground bore evidence of it (he was still learning to control his excitement). Bear's family had called me to help guide them in the right direction, making sure he was well trained, cooperative and socialised.

Bear was well trained already. At this infantile age, he would sit for his food, walk beside his owners, come when called and happily retire to his crate each night for bedtime. This was textbook perfection. The only thing left to do was socialise him.

So I let my own staffy, Chester, out of the car and allowed Bear to approach him. Chester has always been a pushover with puppies. He lets them crawl all over him, chase his tail and lick the tongue right out of his mouth. Chester stood over Bear, as Bear stopped, dropped and rolled in appeasement. The owners expressed their concern for Bear, quickly scooping him up and gently cradling him in their arms, as any human would do for their child in danger. Bear wriggled in confusion and I stood nearby in the same state of mind. What had just happened?

Bear's owners explained to me that they needed to keep him away from all dogs until he was at least four months of age. Chester could make him ill, give him parvo (parvovirus), kennel cough, fleas, mange, ringworm, diarrhoea, hookworm, heartworm – Chester could kill him! They were right. Every puppy book, veterinarian handout and pet shop flyer they had read confirmed their fear. I respected their concern and put Chester back in the car.

It is true that dogs die of parvo. It is a horrendous virus puppies can contract that attacks their digestive system with absolute brutality. Spread from one dog to another, it is usually picked up by direct contact with another dog's infected faeces. After being ingested, the virus spreads through the throat's lymphatic tissue, moving into the bloodstream, where it travels to impose its morbidity on the cells of lymph nodes, intestinal tract and bone marrow. After the destruction of the lymph nodes and intestinal tract tissue, gut bacteria moves into the bloodstream and, at this point, the puppy's body goes into sepsis. In severe cases, parvo is fatal.

Awareness of parvo is understandably one of the main reasons puppy owners do not engage their puppies in socialisation until they are at least four months of age – after their last booster. Hundreds, even thousands, of puppies and dogs die from parvo each year.

However, a puppy's experience of socialisation in its early weeks of life can have a significant influence on their long-term development. If a puppy is completely secluded from other dogs they are far more likely to experience antisocial behaviours as an adult, including aggression and biting. And each year many beloved dogs die as a result of such behaviours. While I am not here to argue that puppies of any age should be thrust upon the disease-ridden world in which we live for the purpose of the odd bum sniff, I do want to put some of the risk into perspective.

Of the 46 500 dogs the RSPCA took in 2015, 6765 were euthanised. A disturbing number, although down from the 19 852 that were put to sleep in 2011. In just four years this organisation has managed to reduce the number of dogs killed by almost two-thirds, which is so incredibly encouraging!

Looking further into the numbers, however, we see that of the 6765 dogs euthanised in 2015, 4700, or 70 per cent of them, lost their life due to 'behavioural issues'. Had the owners of these dogs socialised them properly, would the statistics of euthanasia still look the same? I don't believe they would.

A complicated and loaded issue, I know, intertwined with so many layers of systemic failures, but I cannot speak to all of them. What I can speak to though is my understanding of how owners perceive socialisation and how its importance is regrettably too far down on the priority list of responsible dog ownership.

How can you safely socialise your puppy?

- From the day you meet your puppy, find dog groups in your area who also have puppies and visit their homes
- Create a puppy club, just like a mothers' group (or fathers' group), where you provide opportunities for your puppy to learn how to behave around other dogs
- Find friends who have calm and tolerant older dogs and take your puppy for a visit
- Join a local puppy class and go as often as you can. Get the phone numbers of the other members and catch up in the week for play dates at each others' homes.

Engaging your puppy in positive socialisation will give him the best chance to grow into a calm, cooperative and controlled dog. A dog who is tolerant and confident doesn't react to situations that are unpredictable, because they are able to control their impulses.

So what should your puppy learn through positive socialisation? They should be taught to make good choices when faced with other dogs and other animals. You want to raise a dog who is able to show cooperative behaviours, is confident and is trusting of their leader. The success of this comes down to you.

In a puppy school environment, I like to see puppies of a similar size and age off their leads in a confined area. Allow them to explore and meet each other while you sit on the floor and observe. What can you see? Who is in the corner and more interested in receiving treats? Who is jumping on top of the others even if the others are showing signs of avoidance? Who is sitting on their owner's lap shaking? Each of these puppies is an individual who is telling us something different.

The puppy who is showing signs of tolerance should be immediately rewarded and given an opportunity for space and safety. The antagonising puppy should be removed immediately from that situation and given time to calm down, be taught better impulse control strategies, or perhaps join a group with slightly larger and more energetic dogs. The puppy sitting on their owner's lap shaking should be removed from the class and allowed to sit at a comfortable distance. Perhaps that is in the same room, or maybe it is just outside, where the puppy can hear the others but not be confronted. A good puppy trainer will identify this and find a space where your dog can still experience aspects of socialisation, without discomfort or uncertainty. It is imperative to set your dog up for success before you can start to capture the good stuff that we looked at in the previous chapter.

Once you have discovered what your puppy feels comfortable doing, then you can start to reward them at their individual pace, instead of at yours or your instructor's. I too often see puppy classes run as a generic experience, where many puppies end up learning to be far more antisocial than pro-social during this critical period in their lives. Remember, our dogs cannot control much of their own environment, so if we don't do it for them then we are effectively setting them up for failure. To me, puppy school should be an experience based on the puppy learning pro-social behaviours and the owner understanding who their dog is, how they feel and what they want. If we could graduate puppies and owners with this knowledge, instead of focusing on the basics of the sit and drop, we would have far fewer dangerous incidents with adult dogs.

Does my dog really understand everything I say?

Although I firmly believe we need to start to understand a dog's language more than they need to understand ours, there is some evidence that dogs are superior linguists. Scientists in Hungary using fMRI scanning found that dogs not only understood the meaning of many words, but their meaning via the intonation of our voice. They also discovered that a dog's brain could process familiar words in the same way that we do. They could discriminate the meaning of words with varying intonations, with praising words matched to praising intonations resulting in the most positive response.

These results suggest that dogs can decipher words and intonation as well as combine them to understand their meaning. Whether this ability came about through natural evolution or as selectively bred trait during domestication, there is no doubt that humans and dogs share an incredible ability to understand each other.

Is it too late for my dog?

Getting to know your dog allows you to understand what sort of social experiences are appropriate for them. Some dogs are born with a strong predisposition for timidity and social anxiety. Just one negative social experience can instil a lifelong fear. For others, their predisposition for tolerance and confidence may leave them relatively unshaken after a moment of conflict.

Not every dog is born comfortable interacting with every other dog, and some dogs never learn to feel comfortable. And you know what? That is okay! A good leader listens to their followers and respects their feelings. If you own a dog who just doesn't feel at ease mixing with other dogs, then respect that. Naturally try to empower them in controlled environments and spend time capturing any pro-social behaviours, but at the same time, don't set them up to fail.

We are all living beings on this earth, all struggling to coexist and survive based on what is important to us. The mark of any empathic and positive relationship is that it is based on trust and respect.

If your dog is anxious when you're out for a walk, do a U-turn. If your dog isn't listening to you, become more interesting by increasing your energy, using treats and playing games. If your dog is digging up the yard, take them for a run. Listen to them. Lead them. Love them.

The love you have for your dog may have sound scientific foundations, but it also has sound spiritual foundations – a sense that you want what's best for them, a need to protect them and a belief that together you are happier and healthier.

Give them CPR (consistency, patience and respect), remember the 3 Cs – capture their calm, cooperative and controlled behaviours – and always look after yourself. You owe it to your dog. You owe it to yourself.

Did you know . . . *it has been thought that a man with a dog is more attractive to women, resulting in him being three times more likely to receive a phone number from a potential love interest? The most successful wingman is a labrador. Sadly, the least successful is thought to be a bull terrier.*

9.

Motivation

'Motivation is the art of getting people to do what you want them to do because they want to do it.'

Dwight D Eisenhower

One of the most difficult things to do is motivate people.

One of the easiest things to do is motivate dogs.

Closely tied in with our desires and needs, motivation is the engine of our behaviours and drives us to reach the goals we set in life. It is an interesting force because while it can be easy to find, it can be just as easily lost.

Motivation is about investing effort and time into something that reaps a reward. By nature, the less effort required and the quicker the reward there is for us, the better. This makes complete sense.

Think for a moment about animals in the wild. They don't have the luxury of knowing when their next meal might come, so they need to conserve as much energy as possible. Instinctively, humans are still wild. We crave foods high in fat and sugar because our bodies tells us they will keep us alive. We don't want to unnecessarily expend effort because energy is precious. If we need to use a huge amount of energy for a small resource, we will spend time trying to find a better way to obtain it that takes less effort and wastes less energy.

What about when a reward is not directly in front of us? This requires even more motivation . . . a lot more! I am sure you have been in the situation where you have had a New Year's resolution to get fit, to drink less, to study more, or whatever is important in your life, but after days, weeks or months, you just stop. The motivation is lost because the reward seems too far off and difficult to achieve. It takes too much effort and no longer has the power over you that it once did.

Dog training can feel similarly difficult at times. It is a hard slog that demands long-range motivation. However, although it requires mutual motivation between you and your dog, it does not require equal motivation. The person needs to initiate it, keep it going and follow through each day. The dog just needs to turn up, which they will do, because they have no choice.

DELAYED GRATIFICATION

Research conducted over the past few decades has analysed the motivations of children and teenagers, with a focus on a child's self-efficacy in achieving goals. These studies have established a link between a child's sense of their own ability and their motivation levels to achieve well in school. They have also found that those who have a more positive outlook on themselves feel they have greater control over their learning. Furthermore, they have established that engaging activities result in more engaged individuals and better learning outcomes.

These findings can be applied to all of us, including our dogs. Our perception of self and our sense of confidence and ability can dramatically influence whether we want to engage in an activity or not. What's more, our sense of confidence can be the difference between giving something a go and never trying. Deciding not to try can fuel a cycle of self-doubt and motivation levels that only spiral south. Ultimately, we are the driving (or dragging) force behind our own achievements.

As adults, our developed frontal lobe enables us to think ahead. We can see that immediate sacrifices may reap great benefits in the future. However, children's frontal lobes are not fully connected, with much of the insulating 'copper' protecting their neurons and improving communication efficiency underdeveloped.

Many studies since the 1960s have examined children's brain development, particularly with regard to the area that processes planning, rationalisation and problem solving. Early research tested children's motivation to control their impulses in order to receive a later reward – a process called delayed gratification. In one study, children were offered a marshmallow immediately or two marshmallows if they waited for a short period of time. Called the Marshmallow Test (for obvious reasons), a third of the children waited long enough to get the second reward. Older children were more likely to wait, aligning with the theory of frontal lobe development.

Longitudinal studies showed that children who demonstrated motivation to control their impulses and wait for the two marshmallows were more likely to achieve higher scores in academic tests in their late teens than those who immediately gobbled up the treat once the experimenter had left the room.

Interestingly, some studies have found correlations between self-control and a person's overall health and longevity.

Children who were reported to have low self-control were found to be more likely to smoke, have substance addictions, drop out of school and even engage in criminal behaviour.

The findings of these studies prompt further reflection on the parallels of a child's cognition and a dog's. Dogs and children are often motivated by the same things:

- How long something takes
- How much energy it requires
- What the benefits are

While dogs have a natural instinct to seek immediate gratification, those who are able to learn self-control and the benefits of delayed gratification are more successful in life. They are less likely to get into fights and more likely to feel a strong sense of self-worth and competency, as well as a positive sense of control.

These dogs will be happier and healthier, with a greater sense of optimism about the benefits of resisting their impulses. Sometimes this optimism is innate and sometimes it must be taught, but usually it's a combination of the two.

HOW OPTIMISTIC IS YOUR DOG?

Research around optimism in dogs has sparked a great deal of interest recently, as we recognise more and more that dogs are intelligent and emotional beings, and that these comrades of ours deserve good health and happiness. One study, led by Dr Melissa Starling from the University of Sydney, researched the positive and negative emotional states of dogs and measured them in a way that was stress-free and non-invasive.

Here's an informal mini-experiment you can do in your own home to quasi-measure your dog's level of optimism:

- Teach your dog to associate a bowl with food
- Next, conduct a series of trials in which your dog learns that when the bowl is on the left-hand side of the room, there will always be food in it, but if on the right-hand side of the room, there will never be food in it
- Once your dog clearly understands the difference, evident in their hesitancy or avoidance of the bowl when placed to the right, move the bowl to the middle of the room
- Watch what happens

What did your dog do? Were they hesitant or dismissive? Did they run straight to it expecting food?

Research shows that dogs who enthusiastically move to the bowl in the middle of the room expecting food are more optimistic of a positive outcome. The dogs who are dismissive or uncertain are considered less optimistic.

If your dog was unsure, it doesn't mean that their dog-nitive therapist will be knocking on your door to deliver a diagnosis for depression, it just means that they may need some assistance from you to see the brighter shades over the greys in their world.

HOW CAN YOU MAKE YOUR DOG MORE OPTIMISTIC AND MOTIVATED?

We can improve our dog's optimism by setting achievable goals. The more achievable a goal is, the more motivated they are. Of the vast differences between man and dog, there can be no doubt that our motivations, as primitive as they may be, are remarkably similar. For me, this is encouraging, because it means that when we can understand our dogs, we can understand ourselves.

Goals that are set beyond our reach or our dog's reach should be avoided at all cost. Some marketing and business strategists may disagree however, believing instead that setting the bar higher than usual pushes people beyond their limits even if the overall goal isn't met. This may be true.

However, when we cannot reach a goal, we begin to consider failure. Remember that there is a great difference between failing at something and being set up for failure. I believe failure is essential to success. Setting unachievable goals, however, is setting yourself up for failure. If something is too hard, we consider failure more excusable and acceptable, and, even worse, it becomes expected – leaving you with a sense of defeat and worthlessness. So how can you push yourself just enough to improve, without pushing so much that you fail? For ourselves and our dogs, we set achievable goals.

This does not mean that the big achievement you were planning to work towards cannot ever be reached. It simply means that it must be reached through a series of smaller and successive goals. This will set you and your dog up for success from the start.

TRAINING YOUR DOG TO RECALL

Let's say you want to teach your dog to recall (come back to you). What if I said to you, 'Where would you start? It's extremely hard, it takes too long and I don't know if it will work.' This doubt would likely set you and your dog up for failure. If we see a task as too enormous and difficult, it can mean that we will never follow through.

But what if we approached it as forty tiny goals to ultimate success? We could break it down as follows:

1. Goal inside the house

- On-lead, your dog looks at you and you reward them
- On-lead, your dog walks towards you as you walk encouragingly backwards and you reward them
- On-lead, your dog runs towards you as you run away and you reward them when they reach you
- On-lead, your dog walks with you without you luring them and you reward them
- On-lead, your dog focuses on you 90 per cent of the time
- At each stage, after rewarding your dog, immediately release them back to what they were doing

2. Goal in the backyard

- On-lead, your dog looks at you and you reward them
- On-lead, your dog walks towards you as you walk encouragingly backwards and you reward them
- On-lead, your dog runs towards you as you run away and you reward them when they reach you
- On-lead, your dog walks with you without you luring them
- On-lead, your dog focuses on you 95 per cent of the time
- At each stage, after rewarding your dog, immediately release them back to what they were doing

3. Goal in the front yard

- On-lead, your dog looks at you and you reward them
- On-lead, your dog walks towards you as you walk encouragingly backwards and you reward them
- On-lead, your dog runs towards you as you run away and you reward them when they reach you

- On-lead, your dog walks with you without you luring them
- On-lead, your dog focuses on you 100 per cent of the time
- At each stage, after rewarding your dog, immediately release them back to what they were doing

4. Goal at a fenced park on a quiet day

- On-lead, your dog looks at you and you reward them
- On-lead, your dog walks towards you as you walk encouragingly backwards and you reward them
- On-lead, your dog runs towards you as you run away and you reward them when they reach you
- On-lead, your dog walks with you without you luring them
- On-lead, your dog focuses on you 100 per cent of the time
- At each stage, after rewarding your dog, immediately release them back to what they were doing

5. Goal inside the house

- Off-lead, your dog looks at you and you reward them
- Off-lead, your dog walks towards you as you walk encouragingly backwards and you reward them
- Off-lead, your dog runs towards you as you run away and you reward them when they reach you
- Off-lead, your dog walks with you without you luring them
- Off-lead, your dog focuses on you 100 per cent of the time
- At each stage, after rewarding your dog, immediately release them back to what they were doing

6. Goal in the backyard

- Off-lead, your dog looks at you and you reward them
- Off-lead, your dog walks towards you as you walk encouragingly backwards and you reward them
- Off-lead, your dog runs towards you as you run away and you reward them when they reach you
- Off-lead, your dog walks with you without you luring them
- Off-lead, your dog focuses on you 100 per cent of the time
- At each stage, after rewarding your dog, immediately release them back to what they were doing

7. Goal in the front yard

- Off-lead, your dog looks at you and you reward them
- Off-lead, your dog walks towards you as you walk encouragingly backwards and you reward them
- Off-lead, your dog runs towards you as you run away and you reward them when they reach you
- Off-lead, your dog walks with you without you luring them
- Off-lead, your dog focuses on you 100 per cent of the time
- At each stage, after rewarding your dog, immediately release them back to what they were doing

8. Goal at a fenced park on a quiet day

- Off-lead, your dog looks at you and you reward them
- Off-lead, your dog walks towards you as you walk encouragingly backwards and you reward them
- Off-lead, your dog runs towards you as you run away and you reward them when they reach you

- Off-lead, your dog walks with you without you luring them
- Off-lead, your dog focuses on you 100 per cent of the time
- At each stage, after rewarding your dog, immediately release them back to what they were doing

There are forty achievable goals here instead of one big demotivating goal. By breaking something up and exhibiting self-control and consistency, you and your dog can achieve anything.

The most important part: always release your dog immediately from the recall so they can go back to what they were doing (if safe). Usually, the only time owners call their dogs is when they want to end the fun. Start to become part of the fun instead. Dogs don't return to boring owners or owners who punish them.

You will encounter many bumps and minor setbacks during the journey of dog training. Even with smaller goals such as the above, failure may still occur at a certain step. If you don't achieve what you set out to the first time, then that's okay – in fact, that can be an essential part of greater success.

I have a Winston Churchill quote up in my office: 'Success is stumbling from failure to failure without losing your enthusiasm.' It's something I live by each and every day.

REWARDING YOUR DOG

In dog-training land, we replace the word 'reward' with 'reinforcer'. They mean the same thing, but we like to use words with more syllables. The reinforcer is what your dog is motivated by and there is a general equation we work by:

stimulus + reinforcement = behaviour occurs again

stimulus + punishment = behaviour goes extinct

The effect of reinforcement on a dog's mindset can be seen in 'Pavlovian conditioning', in which a neutral stimulus (something that has no meaning to the dog) is paired with something that has inherent meaning (something the dog is naturally motivated by, such as food). This is called an unconditioned stimulus. When these stimuli are paired together, the othrwise neutral stimulus begins to have meaning.

Example

Let's say the neutral stimulus is the word 'yes!' and the unconditioned stimulus is food or play.

If you say the word 'yes!' to a dog, it probably has no meaning.

To create an association, immediately (within one or two seconds) give them a treat after the word 'yes!'

Say the word again and reward. Repeat this several times.

Next, try to repeat the word 'yes' with minimal distractions, pairing it with a treat each time.

Soon, the word becomes associated with a reward. You will know your dog has made the association when you say the word 'yes' and they come to you with the expectation of getting rewarded.

'Clicker training' is a form of Pavlovian conditioning, whereby we build an association between the neutral stimulus (i.e. a meaningless sound) with the unconditioned stimulus (i.e. food). All of a sudden the dog equates the sound with food.

Another form of conditioning is known as 'operant conditioning'. An example of this could be when a dog is cued to sit. When they sit, they get rewarded and if they don't sit, they don't get rewarded. There becomes an association just like with Pavlovian conditioning, but the main difference is that the behaviour is contingent on the consequence. Pavlovian conditioning creates responses and reactions to stimuli, where with operant conditioning, we tend to be looking for particular behaviours. In all my training, I use a combination of both learning principles.

Punishment, like failure, is often a stigmatised word because it is not completely understood. The truth is, life is full of punishments. By definition, a punishment is simply a stimulus either added or removed, with the goal of causing the extinction of a behaviour. My ethical standpoint on dog training is that is should be based on empowerment, trust and respect. This does not mean that I have never punished a dog, but it does mean that I never put a dog in a situation in which they will fail, or come to any harm.

The above principles of learning are based on science, and while I respect that 'positive punishment' (physical or verbal correction such as raising your voice, yanking the dog's collar or standing over the dog with intimidation) is effective in extinguishing unwanted behaviours, I also believe that there is a better way, which is to understand your dog well enough that you don't put them in that situation in the first place. Remember that while you should never be afraid to fail, setting our dogs up to fail creates confusion and anxiety for them, because only one of you will ever have complete control over this world and it will never be them.

When we encourage and support our dogs to succeed, it's essential to acknowledge their accomplishments with reinforcers. Effectively, a reinforcer is something that they are most motivated by at that exact moment. It's all about giving them this reward as quickly and easily as possible.

So what is a good reward for your dog? It's not always food. Don't fall for that trap. There are many things your dog wants, you just need to observe and find out what they are. With a pen and paper, write down a list of things your dog loves. Here are some examples of rewards that your dog may love:

- Treats
- Being allowed inside
- Sitting on my lap
- Being on the couch
- Going for a run
- Going to the beach
- Being scratched under the chin
- Feeling safe
- Playing tug of war
- Being chased when they have a ball
- Fetching a stick from the water
- Getting the last bit of your toast
- Travelling in the car
- Agility courses

To successfully reward your dog, you should match their good behaviour with the most suitable reinforcer at that particular moment.

Example

If your dog sits patiently outside your back door, what would reinforce this behaviour? If you said 'being allowed inside', I'd say you'd be right!

If you said 'getting a treat and being allowed inside', you'd be right too!

In fact, combining the two rewards may make them even more likely to sit patiently at the door next time.

What if you went outside to give your dog a treat and then closed the door behind you again? It might reinforce their behaviour for a short time, but the treat was not what they really wanted – they wanted to be let inside. Owners often think that a reward is a food treat, but it is rarely that simple.

Look at these scenarios and see if you can figure out the reinforcer. Remember: ask yourself what your dog wants at that exact moment.

BEHAVIOUR	REINFORCER
1. Your dog sits patiently at the base of the couch	
2. Your dog sits at the front door before your walk	
3. Your dog chooses to go and lie on their bed	
4. Your dog heels beside you on a walk	
5. Your dog sees another dog barking at them across the road	

Suggested answers.
1. Allow the dog to jump on the couch 2. Open the door and begin your walk 3. Give them a yummy treat and praise then leave them be. 4. Continue walking, including food here and there if necessary 5. Praise your dog and do a U-turn.

Now, look back at the example we saw earlier of teaching a dog to come when called. If you were training your own dog to do this, which of the reinforcers you wrote out earlier would you use to reward their cooperation?

If you have a puppy who needs to learn to recall or a dog who after years of trying still won't recall, then break up your goal into achievable steps, use your list of reinforcers, watch your dog, observe your surroundings and accomplish one goal at a time.

If your dog reliably comes when called, then think of something else you want to train them to do. Write down a step-by-step achievable plan and use the list of reinforcers to accomplish your goals together.

Whether the goal is for you or your dog, create a timeline that is practicable. Having unrealistic timelines pushes you back to those feelings of disempowerment. Put yourself in a position of strength, power and positivity. The only person who can tell you that you will fail is yourself.

Now let's look at a complete set of achievable steps that incorporate reinforcers to help change your dog's behaviour. While I've used the example of an anxious dog, you can customise the steps to help with any behaviour.

TRAINING YOUR DOG TO FEEL LESS NERVOUS AROUND OTHER DOGS

Note: Any training of reactive or aggressive dogs should be carried out with a qualified dog behaviourist.

Goal 1

Start inside the house.

1. Put your dog on-lead if necessary, and when they look at you, *reinforce* it. Repeat as required.
2. Walk backwards away from your dog with encouragement and when they walk towards you, *reinforce* it. Repeat as required.
3. Keep your dog on lead if necessary and say with enthusiasm, 'There's a dog!' then *reinforce* it. Note: there are no other dogs, you are just trying to pair the words with a reward.
4. Repeat this process several times over ten minutes.

This goal has been reached once your dog understands that focusing on you and the words 'There's a dog!' results in a reward.

Goal 2

Repeat goal 1 but this time in the backyard under some distraction.

1. Put your dog on-lead if necessary, and when they look at you, *reinforce* it. Repeat as required.
2. Walk backwards away from your dog with encouragement and when they walk towards you, *reinforce* it. Repeat as required.
3. Keep your dog on lead if necessary and say with enthusiasm, 'There's a dog!' then *reinforce* it.
4. Repeat this process several times over ten minutes.

This goal has been reached once your dog understands that focusing on you and the words 'There's a dog!' results in a reward.

Goal 3

Repeat goal 2 but this time in the front yard or somewhere under slight distraction.

1. Put your dog on-lead if necessary, and when they look at you, *reinforce* it. Repeat as required.
2. Walk backwards away from your dog with encouragement and when they walk towards you, *reinforce* it. Repeat as required.
3. Keep your dog on-lead if necessary and say with enthusiasm, 'There's a dog!' then *reinforce* it.
4. Repeat this process several times over ten minutes.

This goal has been reached once your dog understands that focusing on you and the words 'There's a dog!' results in a reward.

Goal 4

Repeat goal 3 but this time get a friend who has a well-socialised dog to help out. Visit a neutral location on a quiet day – with your friend's dog at a comfortable distance (below your dog's threshold).

1. When your dog focuses on you under distraction, reinforce it.
2. Walk backwards away from your dog with encouragement and when they walk towards you, *reinforce* it.
3. Keep your dog on-lead and when they see another dog at a distance that they are comfortable with say, 'There's a dog!' then *reinforce*. Remember to include safety as a reinforcer in this step by moving your dog away. Set them up for success.
4. Repeat this process several times over ten minutes.

Note: Make sure you are in a position to remove your dog safely and immediately if another dog violates their threshold. Ensure your dog's limitations are never pushed.

What should you do if you find that your dog doesn't want to work for food? If your dog is not food-motivated it will most likely be because they are anxious and frightened at the time. What can you do to change this? Provide a training environment where your dog feels safe and unafraid and ensure your dog is healthy. Try other rewards such as toys, tugs and praise. Each dog is different and finding the right reinforcer may require some trial and error.

THE BEST BEHAVIOURS TO TRAIN

Ultimately, we want to motivate our dogs to embody the 3 Cs: *calm*, *cooperative* and *controlled* behaviours and mindsets.

Every time your dog is at ease around other dogs, you have motivated them through setting up and rewarding their *calm* state of mind.

Whenever you achieve any small goal, you have motivated them to *cooperate*. You are capturing and reinforcing the good moments by empowering them and knowing exactly what it is that they want in exchange.

Every goal you achieve means that you have motivated your dog to show controlled behaviours.

Reinforcing the 3 Cs makes you an excellent dog trainer and better yet, it makes you an inspiring dog leader.

INTERMITTENT REINFORCEMENT

Have you ever thought *my dog won't listen to me unless I have food*? Don't worry, you're not alone. At least half of my clients have felt this at some stage and its easily overcome through what's called an intermittent schedule of reinforcement. In other words, we make the rewards random.

Sometimes the rewards are big, sometimes they're small and sometimes there's no reward at all. The more our dog thinks there is a chance at winning something big, the more motivated they are.

Intermittent reinforcements are highly motivating. So much so that this random rewards system can cause us to go above and beyond any normal behaviour, on the chance that there is a jackpot around the corner waiting for us.

An example of the intermittent schedule of reinforcement in humans is gambling. According to the Productivity Commission's report into gambling (2011), almost 80 per cent of Australians engage in gambling. This statistic suggests we are among the biggest gamblers in the world. In fact, gambling is so addictive that almost half a million Aussies are at moderate risk of problem gambling, costing the country over $4.5 billion a year. It is only too clear how intermittent reinforcement can cause a behaviour to occur again and again without stopping.

Inadvertently providing intermittent reinforcement is an issue that parents encounter on a daily basis with their children. After what may feel like an eternity of crying, tantrums and insolence, parents can feel that it's easier give in to the persistent demands of their child. Ironically, caving in to the child's unwanted behaviours every now and then only ensures that they will create a scene the next time they don't get that chocolate bar at the checkout. Just as intermittent reinforcement can assist us to train behaviours we want, conversely, it can train and even cement behaviours we do not want.

This is why it's so important in dog training to intermittently reinforce good behaviours and to consistently *not* reinforce the bad ones.

SUMMARY

Most dog behaviours can be modified if not managed through behaviour change on both our end and theirs. One interesting approach to achieving this is capturing or seizing the very moment your dog offers to do something good. There are three main emotional states and behaviours that I feel are most important to capture and they are when your dog is calm, cooperative and controlled. Your dog doesn't need to be expressing all of these at once for a reward, but the more the better.

One common mistake owners make in dog training is not understanding what their dog actually wants in exchange for these behaviours. This can often make training difficult and unsuccessful. Remember, there are numerous reinforcers for your dog. Get to know your dog's motivations and emotions and soon you will be able to read their mind just as well as they can read yours.

Did you know . . . *the most popular New Year's resolutions are to get fit and healthy? According Nielsen (2016), only 8 per cent of those surveyed followed through with their resolution. Research shows that those who set resolutions that are achievable in the short term are far more likely to be kept. Imagine what you could achieve if you set achievable goals, step by step!*

10.

Who's Rescued Who?

CASE STUDY

If you love staffies you would have loved Freddie. A brindle-coloured character with four white socks worn high like a private school boy and an asymmetrical blaze that ran from the top of his head to the tip of his nose. A tongue that he had never grown into hung out to the side of his mouth, where a set of teeth might have once been and he had a smile that would make anyone's heart melt. He was rugged and full of life.

Born and bred in the country, Freddie roamed free from property to property, profiting from the leftovers other dogs had ignored in their bowls, resting in neighbours beds along the way and foraging in the chicken pens for freshly laid eggs.

He was as close to a wild dog as you could get, and whilst his owners might have cared for him the best way they knew how, Freddie had only one care in the world, and that was himself.

Whilst the freedom of the country may sound appealing to many, when the wild meets civilisation, they don't always mix. Freddie had many quirky habits, but perhaps the most unusual was his obsession for chasing the train each day. Each morning like clockwork, the country train would power through the town, and as it religiously swept by, so too would Freddie. Chasing it with all his might, Freddie would relentlessly prey upon the carriage, and whilst he never caught it, it never deterred him from trying the next time.

It was not just a hobby for Freddie, it was an obsession and after what may have been years of determined practice to defeat the train, Freddie eventually fell victim to the game. As the train had motioned towards him, Freddie waited for its approach and like always, ran along side it. This time however, Freddie's timing was off and he found himself under the train rather than alongside it. He found his body between the tracks and the train and as it left, his leg went with it.

Freddie would have died that day if it weren't for Anne and Rob, who saw the incident unfold before their eyes. They picked Freddie up in their baby's blanket and rushed him to the local vet. He stayed there for two weeks and over all that time, nobody came to enquire about him or claim him as theirs. This time, Freddie really was on his own. By this point, I usually get a phone call.

Freddie recovered eventually and whilst he may have lost his leg, you would have thought he didn't know. I brought him home and helped him through rehabilitation in the hope I could help him find the perfect home. Freddie lived with us for three months. He learnt to balance his body properly and build muscle to support himself. He had been wild for so long that the only way he knew to get what he needed was to control it.

Freddie would growl at me if I touched his collar and if I was anywhere near his food, he would have taken my leg too if he could. He was an exquisite challenge. I learnt a lot about how important CPR was through this dog. I also learnt how valuable it was to capture good behaviours when they were already happening. When Freddie volunteered to sit, he was praised. When he allowed me near him after he had eaten, he got treats. When he showed patience, he got my attention. Soon, Freddie learnt that everything he wanted and more could come from me. All he needed to do was be calm, cooperative and controlled. Freddie became the best student I have ever had. I think I became his best student too.

Whilst there were many moments during his rehab where I wasn't sure if he could be adopted, one day, he showed me that he could be just like any other dog. But he wasn't. To me, he was even better. Freddie was the type of dog who just made you feel that you had earned his respect. He had this way of making you feel good about yourself. He was ready.

Jessica, the vet nurse who had helped Freddie recover from his injury, also volunteered at the local elderly citizens centre. She had developed a friendship with an older gentleman, Pat, who visited the facility each Friday for some company. He had fought in Vietnam and worked as a mechanic in his younger years. In some ways, he was a little like Freddie; independent and capable but in need of someone to care for him.

Jessica had mentioned Pat to me before and I knew that Pat and Freddie were a perfect match. One Friday, I brought Freddie up to the centre and just like a dream come true, Freddie and Pat fell in love.

If you know anything about staffies, you will know how they have a habit of leaning against you. It's almost as if they are leaning against you in approval. Whilst it is probably a needy behaviour, for Pat, it melted his heart. Freddie immediately walked up to Pat and without discrimination or judgement, leant against his leg. Pat reached down to touch Freddie and within minutes, Freddie had made himself comfortable on his new master's lap.

That day, Freddie went home with Pat. That was five years ago and to this day, Pat still visits his group of friends at the facility each Friday. But now he has a friend who accompanies him. Pat reports regularly to Jessica how Freddie was never a rescue. Instead it was he who needed rescuing. In some ways, Pat says that Freddie saved his life.

There is something about rescuing a dog that automatically certifies you as a good person. Rescue dogs often come with baggage, anxiety, fears and destructive tendencies. Often they are not socialised and are reactive. Instead of the blank canvas a puppy provides, they are a canvas coloured in bold and recalcitrant patterns, so chaotic that it can leave us wondering why we bought the painting in the first place.

As with any dog, look to the principles in Chapter 1–3, in particular the 3 Cs and CPR. They will help your rescue dog settle into their new life with you, and set them up for success in the future. And if you've rescued an older dog, Chapter 15 will show you how these techniques can be just as effective for them with some small adjustments.

Someone who makes the sacrifice to rescue a dog is someone who knows it is the right thing to do. They want to save a life, protect an animal from pain and suffering and give them the love they deserve but may never have had. One of the things I adore about many rescue organisations is their rigorous vetting of potential adopters. You have to prove that you can provide the dog with all the things they need so that they are never subjected to the uncontrollable and unpredictable environment of a shelter ever again. There is an undeniable passion about people who work for these organisations and I am in awe of their efforts.

A rescue dog may bring along the baggage of a troubled past, but it is soon overshadowed by the remarkable bond you share with a rescue dog. There is something about enduring suffering that makes one so grateful for its absence. The exposure to cold winters makes the simplicity of being indoors so comforting. The routine of food excites one who never knew when their next meal might come. Rescue dogs remind us of the simplicity of life; how fortunate we are to have basic comforts such as shelter, food and water.

These dogs who have come from nothing look into our eyes and thank us. I know my own rescue dog, Alma, is grateful. She may live in the now, but she hasn't forgotten her past. Those of you who have adopted a shelter dog will understand what I mean. Alma looks deep into my soul often and it strikes me that these dogs who we find, in many ways, end up finding us. Alma reminds me of what is important each and every day. She knows exactly who I am and she still loves me. For all my flaws, she stands beside me, because despite all her shortcomings I have stuck by her side too, and I will be right there beside her until the day she leaves us for good.

SEARCH AND RESCUE

With the unique ability to discriminate scents with such high acuity, dogs have been employed across the world to search for and rescue human beings. In Australia, highly trained and accredited dogs are deployed for a range of jobs including detection of scents, tracking, disaster rescue and water searches.

A famous dog of our time was Bretagne, the last surviving search and rescue dog of 9/11, who passed away in 2016.

Among 300 other talented and determined canines, Bretagne assisted in the location of several people buried under the remnants of the twin towers.

Bretagne went on to assist in the aftermath of many hurricanes also, including Katrina and Rita, and later boosted the confidence of countless school children by providing non-judgemental ears to those learning to read. Dogs are amazing. Their motivation to work for us, to please us and to be by our side is what makes them our very best friends. Who on earth sticks by our side like a dog?

Those of you who have rescued a dog, thank you. Each of the hundreds of thousands who have made this sacrifice deserve great acknowledgement. You have saved a life, perhaps even more than one, and without you the future of these animals would be uncertain at the very least. But the truth is, this sacrifice is a privilege. Among the gratitude, unconditional love and loyalty of those we save, we find that often they are the ones who end up saving us.

SUMMARY

Although adopting a dog from a rescue shelter is effectively saving a life, many report that the experience is mutual. Looking into the eyes of the one you have saved can generate emotions similar to those of parental love. If you are looking to bring a dog into your family, adoption is without a doubt the most earnest of choices and one that may awaken your sense of gratitude and altruism. A rescue will make you a better person.

11.

Loyalty

There is nobody on this blue and green earth who is as loyal as a dog. Nobody is as excited by your presence and content to just be by your side at every waking moment. Here we have an animal whose entire life is dedicated to us. And as indisputably devoted as they are, I wonder if we deserve it.

Some may say that this loyalty is in fact simply an expression of a dog's neediness; that they merely stick by our side because they can't survive without us. Perhaps their need to trail behind us, to sit at our side and to gaze into our eyes is nothing more than manipulation – they know we provide their resources, therefore their faithfulness is simply thoughtful exploitation. But within every inch of my being, I don't believe that's all there is. For me, the loyalty of a dog is much deeper. It goes beyond science and enters the realm of the unexplainable.

CASE STUDY

Her name was Charlotte. A corgi with legs just inches long and four paws facing ninety degrees from where they should be. She was one of those dogs who would come and sit on you, nudge her head under your hand and fall asleep in your arms. She needed to touch you, lean against you or be within your view.

I was called to meet Charlotte after an accident that not only cost the earth in repairs for her owner but one that almost claimed her life. Charlotte had split open her front paws and severely cut her face and neck after jumping through a glass window when left home alone one day.

On that day, the trail of bloody pawprints through the house gave away much of her motivations, as did the blood spatter on the broken glass. Charlotte's owner, Neil, had returned home after a longer day at work than expected and soon discovered the horrific scene after Charlotte greeted him at the front door. Usually, Charlotte would be faithfully waiting outside for Neil when he arrived home from work. But on this day, she had figured out how to get just that little bit closer, even if it meant risking her life.

Understandably, Neil was incredibly concerned. He and Charlotte had been in each other's lives since his wife had passed away and they had come to rely on each other for companionship. Wherever Neil went, Charlotte faithfully followed. From room to room, in the shower, the toilet, the kitchen; she was his shadow, night and day.

When I met Neil and Charlotte, I was immediately struck by how nervous Charlotte was. She barked and lunged at me, full of empty threats. She was extraordinarily spooked by my presence and I realised that Neil and Charlotte didn't have many visitors.

In fact, I was the first visitor they had had since Neil's wife had died three months prior.

Neil talked to me about Charlotte, each time looking at her in adoration. There was a loyalty there that is rare and one I am not that lucky to see all the time. It was a complete and total mutual dedication. But just as the devotion to one another glued them together, the bond was overwhelmingly part of the problem. To Charlotte, Neil was her entire existence. She was completely dependent on him and without him in view, she panicked. Neil was no different towards her.

Charlotte's paws were bandaged and her head in an Elizabethan Collar whilst she sat beside Neil on the couch. I explained to Neil that I admired his devotion to Charlotte, but the devotion had become overbearing, with Charlotte suffering greatly as a result. I continued to say that sometimes, we rely on our dog's loyalty and companionship to fulfil our own needs, without realising that we are inadvertently reinforcing neediness and anxiety in our dogs. I could see Neil's eyes fill with tears, but he understood completely. He began to cry and then apologised to Charlotte whose head collected the gentle tears as they fell from Neil's eyes.

That's the thing about separation behaviour, nobody ever intends to cause harm to their dog. In fact, separation anxiety usually occurs because dog owners give more love, more dedication, more indulgence than a dog can handle.

Neil promised me that he would stop encouraging Charlotte to follow him and that he would work on providing a predictable routine for her so that she felt safe when he was not home. I was impressed by Neil's intuition and willingness to change, at the expense of his own needs, so I let him in on a little secret.

I asked Neil where Charlotte sleeps at night. Neil immediately hung his head like a child in trouble and told me that she slept on his bed. He explained that she always asks for permission to jump on the bed and that he doesn't mind her being there, despite what dog trainers might recommend. I smiled and told him that despite popular belief there is no evidence to suggest that allowing your dog to sleep on your bed leads to bad behaviour or poor hygiene. In fact, research shows there is a correlation between a dog sleeping on your bed and better behaviour due to a close bond between dog and owner.

Once the confessions were out, I asked Neil if Charlotte was destructive in the house. Neil immediately shook his head and told me that she had never done so much as sniff the edge of the couch. My eyes lit up as I began to give him a tip that could help to change Charlotte's life whilst Neil was at work.

'Get a dog door, Neil, and let Charlotte have access to your bed during the day.' I said.

Neil looked at me perplexed. These were two things that he had always thought were big no-nos. 'Allow your dog inside when you're not home? Allow your dog on your bed when you're not home?' He asked. And I simply replied 'Yep.'

Let's think about Charlotte for a moment. What is driving her to risk her life and get inside the house? Amongst the answers were her need for familiarity, predictability, control, safety, routine and comfort. Being able to access her safe place was what she needed.

Neil promised me he would get a dog door and that he would try my suggestion. We shook on it and I left, hoping he would follow through with his end of the bargain. Before I even arrived back to my office, Neil had called me from the hardware store in excitement that he had found the perfect-sized doggy door and told me he was going to spend the rest of the afternoon setting up Charlotte's new personal entrance. For me, it is so elating to hear the excitement in a client's voice when they feel they have direction and hope for a positive outcome.

One week went by, then two weeks and I hadn't heard from Neil. By the start of the third week I wondered what had happened, but always make a point not to call clients because any behaviour change has to come from them, not me. Neil didn't call, but sent me an email with the subject heading: We have a problem.

That's something nobody wants to read when opening an email, let alone from someone who has paid you for your services! With great hesitation, I clicked on the email, eyes squinted in the hope the bad news would hit me more gently. The email opened with a picture of Charlotte. The only text to caption the photo was 'this is what I came home to'.

The picture loaded on my computer and it was certainly a picture of Charlotte. But no blood, no bandages, no broken glass. It was Charlotte on Neil's bed, all four paws in the air, eyes barely open and Neil's face photo-bombing with a smile wider than Luna Park's entrance. It had worked. Charlotte was safe and Neil was over the moon with gratitude. I was so happy to see them both able to get on with their lives together. I wanted to take the credit for this ingenious suggestion, but in all honesty, the credit had to go to Charlotte.

Charlotte had told me exactly what she needed and so I just came up with an answer. When we listen to what our dogs are trying to say, we can find simple ways to solve what seem to be the most complex of problems. Charlotte often features in photos sent to me from Neil. They are usually images of her in the most relaxed poses around the house along with captions that tell me how happy she is. Often Neil features in them too, but with a confused facial expression as he tries to figure out if the photo has been taken or not.

Research shows people in close and fulfilling relationships are the most loyal. It makes sense, doesn't it? We want to follow, to think of and to dedicate ourselves to those who make us feel that our time and effort is worth it. Dogs are great at this. They make us feel appreciated and loved. They show great sadness during our absences and ecstatic happiness upon our return. But do we love our dogs because they are loyal or is it simply because on a subconscious level they give us an ego boost? I am not entirely sure, but if it were purely an ego boost, our interest would eventually wane.

Perhaps this is the difference between those who continue to love and care for their dog across a lifetime and those who tire from their dog's ongoing dependence, resulting in the mass of puppies dumped at shelters each year. While there are sometimes extenuating circumstances that result in people having to surrender their dog, often there aren't, and I think we need to improve education to shift the perception many have of animals from animated objects to sentient comrades.

FAMOUS LOYAL FRIENDS

Let's look at some stories from around the world that exemplify the remarkable loyalty between dogs and their owners.

Capitán

In 2005, within the Cordoba province of Argentina, a shepherd mix named Capitán was gifted to Damian Guzman as a thirteenth birthday present by his father, Miguel.

In 2006, Miguel Guzman died suddenly, leaving a grieving family of not just humans, but a dog too. This dog suffered deeply with the loss of his master and in distress left his family and was nowhere to be found. On a visit to Miguel's gravesite just days after the funeral, the Guzman family found their missing dog. He had not jumped the fence and wondered aimlessly down a highway or escaped to play with the neighbour next door, he had gone looking for Miguel. Capitán had somehow located the cemetery and then the very site where his master was laid to rest. The family said that when Capitán greeted them that day, he was barking and wailing as if he was crying in grief. Although they attempted to bring him home many times, Capitán unfailingly returned to his master's side each night.

The cemetery director, Hector Baccega, told journalists that Capitán would wander around the cemetery often, exploring his surroundings, but each evening as the clock ticked over to six, he would faithfully return to Miguel. He said that the dog would lay on top of the grave each night, almost as if he were there to keep Miguel company and to protect him.

Recent reports say that Capitán still stands vigil over Miguel's place of rest and is cared for by the staff of the cemetery so that he will never have to leave the side of the man he continues to honour.

The universality of loyalty has been documented throughout the ages. Our very own Australian identity is based on this romance of mateship, sacrifice and camaraderie. As a civilised social species, humans have believed that this remarkable capacity to invest in a relationship is unique to us. But the story of Capitán is one of many examples where dogs trump our own loyalty. His sacrifice and devotion goes beyond what any human would make.

Capitán shows us how important it is to remember to respect and acknowledge those who are in our lives and those we have lost. There is not a moment to be taken for granted. Each opportunity you have to tell someone you love them, you should.

Our time together with those we love must be cherished, for we never know when it will be our last.

Hachikō

Another dog, born in 1923, continues to spark discussions of canine loyalty all over the world. Born on a farm near the town of Odate in Japan, Hachikō was an Akita, a breed known for their large and dignified presence.

Hidesaburo Ueno, a professor at the University of Tokyo, adopted Hachikō as a pet and brought him to the city. The dog faithfully displayed his affection each day when greeting his master upon his return from work. However, unlike our housebound dogs, Hachikō was never confined by gates or fences, so would walk to the Shibuya Station to greet Professor Ueno each day without fail as he disembarked from the train carriage.

The routine greeting was reported to have lasted as long as a year, before Ueno died suddenly of a brain haemorrhage and never returned home. That day and every day after, Hachikō waited for his master at the train station at the exact time he was scheduled to arrive. He continued this for nine years until meeting his own death at the age of twelve.

He has been immortalised in statue form outside Shibuya Station as a symbol of indescribable faithfulness. Cremated and laid by his owner's side, Hachikō will forever be with Professor Ueno, the person he lived for, whose return he yearned for and who he grieved for each and every day for the rest of his life.

Masha

During a blisteringly cold Siberian winter, a dachshund mix named Masha attended Novosibirsk Hospital with her master after he had suddenly fallen ill. With no family to care for him, Masha's master was required to stay at the ward long term, with Masha his only visitor. Masha walked to the hospital on her own accord every day for over a year, retiring to her home by night.

In 2013, Masha's owner died at the hospital, leaving the dog not only physically lost as she tried to find her great love, but also emotionally, never to see him again.

One wonders what dogs like Masha go through. Do they ever truly understand their loss? Can we ever truly understand theirs? We seem to forget how dogs feel until they do something remarkable that we can connect with. But they are always feeling and thinking. We share a lot in common with our faithful counterparts, and while we can't be sure how they experience grief, nobody can deny that a dog experiences a full range of emotions we can relate to.

Several attempts to rehome Masha were made. But despite countless kind-hearted offers to adopt her, Masha was officially adopted by the hospital, with the chief physician agreeing she should stay.

You cannot deny the romance of these stories. It confirms everything we want to believe about dogs: that they are devoted, pure and loving animals. That they are examples of everything we want to be better at. They are our teachers, our inspiration and our best friends.

OVERCOMING SEPARATION ANXIETY IN DOGS

Just like Neil, one of the most common issues people face with their dog is separation anxiety. Not only is this a cause of concern to owners, it is also a devastating animal welfare issue. Dogs who suffer from this anxiety are often overwhelmed with fear and frustration, and can become destructive not just to their backyard, but themselves. Charlotte had been so desperate to find safety that she jumped through glass, and sadly, she is just one of many. I have met dogs who have chewed through doors until the pulp of their teeth was exposed and many who simply conceded to laying in their backyard desperately howling for their pack to return. It is heart-wrenching to think that our dogs can experience these emotions on a daily basis.

Separation anxiety does have links to loyalty. Just as in the stories of Hachikō, Masha and Capitán, we see that the dogs in our lives suffer greatly without access to us. We adore their faithfulness and encourage their close companionship because it makes us feel good, but are we really doing what is best for them?

If your dog experiences the emotions of separation anxiety, it is critical you intervene as soon as possible and prevent it from escalating. There is no 'cure' for severe anxieties, so managing your expectations is critical in the success of behaviour modification and management. I have constructed a ten-point process to help you and your dog understand that separation can be an opportunity, rather than detrimental.

1. This step is arguably the most important: *ensure they have access to their safe place.* Often this is your bed. Access to your bed is often all they need.
2. Teach them to station to their bed and stay. Increase the distance in which you walk away from them, making it always positive. Get them used to being away from you gradually without the world ending.
3. Exercise your dog as much as you can before leaving them. In particular, exercise their brain by playing games that involve problem solving.

4. Consistently reward the 3 Cs: *calm*, *cooperative* and *controlled* behaviours. Scatter rewards out of your sight as a regular routine each day.
5. Prevent your dog from following you by dropping rewards as you walk away from them, making your absence a positive thing.
6. Create a routine for your dog that enables them to predict your impending absence but to associate it with relaxation and positivity.
7. Rehearse your routine as often as you can. Leave the house, close the door and then walk back inside again.
8. Never make a fuss of departures. Instead make them positive by offering a high-value reward to your dog. Never make a fuss of arrivals either. Instead, wait until the dog is *calm*, *cooperative* and *controlled*, then acknowledge them.
9. Create positive olfactory associations using scents such as lavender or worn clothes that are left in the safe place that your dog has access to.
10. Discuss your concerns with a qualified behaviourist or veterinarian to see if an anti-anxiety medication may be of assistance.

CHERISHING LOYALTY

While one could devote a whole book to the motivations of loyalty and the psychology behind its benefits and detriments, sometimes we just need to accept that it is simply one of those things that makes our relationships so special. If we remove the science and embrace its romance, loyalty is one of many traits that we can learn from our dogs to help make us a better person. I am continually inspired by dogs and their ability to make us feel special.

We learn through dogs that those around us who are truly devoted to us deserve to be treated the same way. As your dog sits at your feet right now, think about everyone in your life who has stuck by you. Give them a call, open your heart and embrace them with gratitude and love. These are the friends and family who deserve your time, energy and love.

Sometimes they are people, sometimes they are dogs. If you're lucky, they are both.

SUMMARY

We have much to learn from the *canis familiaris* species. Having spent tens of thousands of years faithfully by our side, they know us better than anyone. It is remarkable to think that people are more likely to be faithful to their dogs than their partners; a clear indication that dogs bear superior qualities to our human beloveds. Perhaps if people showed as much enthusiasm for their partner's arrivals, and sadness for their departures, those in vulnerable relationships may realise the importance of loyalty and its place in any successful partnership.

Did you know . . . *the dog has long been a symbol of loyalty? Depicted in portraits across history and most notably during the Renaissance, with Leonardo da Vinci adorning his artworks with the majestic dog as a mark of faithfulness.*

12.
Gratitude

Whenever I watch my dogs basking in the sun, lying on their backs like a couple of pork chops, I am struck by a major difference between us and them: they can so easily experience complete contentment. The sun on their full bellies provides them with pure moments of gratitude. It makes me think about myself and others who aren't so easily satisfied. What's wrong with us?

If you think about your life, it is filled to the brim with external pressures – mortgages, work stress, bills, arguing with partners, illness, to name but a few. The majority of things that keep us up at night are external stressors that often cannot be controlled and certainly don't make us happy. So why do we invest so much energy into them? I think it goes back once again to our innate need to feel in control and to acquire resources. We have an instinctive drive to hunt and gather, but in the modern world all we seem to be able to collect is an overload of materials useless to survival. Perhaps we are mentally conflicted between our primitive past and advanced present.

According to beyondblue, 45 per cent of Australians will experience depression at some point in their lives. Interestingly, people exposed to prolonged periods of low light and cold temperatures are more likely to experience symptoms of depression – this affliction is called seasonal affective disorder (SAD). Across the world, light-therapy rooms have been introduced to alleviate low mood during winter months, particularly in the UK, Scandanavian countries and across Northern Asia.

Light-therapy rooms have also been used for dogs suffering from symptoms suggestive of SAD. Exposure to artificial lights for half an hour a day showed improved mood and behaviour of dogs that displayed sluggish and low-mood behaviours. These behaviours included a reduction of 'accidents' in the house, aggression, neediness and lethargy or low motivation.

Dogs too are susceptible to stress in circumstances out of their control. As studies of dogs in shelters have begun to increase over the years (to better understand their behaviour, welfare and adoptability) several analyses have focused on the levels of cortisol in their system. Cortisol is what's referred to as the 'stress hormone'. During times of acute stress the levels of this hormone elevate and during times of calm it decreases. While many other methods of determining stress can be applied, measuring cortisol is a uniform and objective approach. Results showed that newly arrived dogs in shelters exhibited high cortisol levels, whereas dogs in predictable and loving homes had a comparatively lower reading.

Furthermore, dogs held in shelters for nine days or more also had high cortisol levels, became more reactive to other dogs and exhibited a significantly decreased ability to cope in their environment. Interestingly, human interactions seemed to calm shelter dogs in these studies, with pats, play and even passive presence reducing levels of the stress hormone. It is refreshing to see that while dogs are renowned for their incredible abilities to reduce our stress levels and makes us feel more grateful, there are times in which we can reciprocate.

Thinking about all the dogs in shelters across the world, experiencing high amounts of stress, does make my cortisol levels rise a little too. But that's the thing about people. We really are not that different to dogs. As mammals, we share much of the same DNA.

Interestingly, cortisol is lowest in people who thrive in leadership positions. This suggests a correlation between success and an ability to cope well with stress. While not all of us are natural-born leaders, there are ways to learn how to manage stress, making us more adaptable and more able to successfully take on leadership roles. If we can learn to cope with the unpredictable and uncontrollable in our lives and find coping strategies that enable us to think logically and clearly, we become someone that others want to follow. In particular, we can become somebody our dogs will look up to. That's the thing about dogs, they will always let you know if you are a leader or, more importantly, if you're not.

Dogs are also able to show you how to cope better with stress. They are the bona fide example of living in the moment, appreciating what is around you and being content with basic necessities. When we consider our materialistic lives, there is nothing we can buy that can guarantee happiness, yet we spend a lifetime chasing after possessions that we eventually leave behind. Dogs are different. They stop and smell the proverbial roses each and every moment they can. Following their example, experiencing gratitude for the simple joys in life is a sure-fire way to reduce stress and find happiness.

The culture of gratitude is quite diverse across the world. In Nepal, accepting a gift with both of your hands indicates the gesture of gratitude. In Japan you would bow, in Russia you would give an odd number of flowers and in China a thank you is more genuine when expressed in actions rather than words. While we may all have different traditions, the sentiment of gratitude is universal. And with it being so widespread, there must be a reason why people from all walks of life continue to search for it within themselves. Does gratitude make us a better person?

Those of us who are able to express gratitude to others tend to benefit from a range of positive outcomes. Research shows a correlation between people who are grateful and general good health. These people tend to exercise more regularly and experience less toxic emotions such as jealousy, resentment and frustration. They also have more positive relationships with others, being able to show sensitivity and empathy, and additionally they experience better self-esteem. They sleep better, eat healthier and live longer. Grateful people have it all.

So how can you be more grateful? I am not sure the problem is that people have forgotten how to feel gratitude – I think it is more that we have lost the time to find it. Let's reconnect with your inner appreciation through the best teacher around: your dog.

YOUR GRATEFUL DOG AND YOU

Stop for a moment, take a mental step backwards and look at your life

Write down all of your favourite people. Your dog already has his list written down in his heart. The people you love and care about are the people you are grateful for. Let them know. You don't have to tell them, you can show them. A hug, a smile, even a gentle touch on their shoulder can let them know they are valued. Your actions have electricity that can transmit to others. Such a simple act can make a huge difference. Dogs are excellent at showing others how they feel. Everything you are prepared to give them, they are grateful for. A walk, a treat, a scratch under the chin. Your praising voice, the small space next to you on the couch, the welcome to come inside and sit with you. Dogs embody gratitude in its purest form. We have so much to learn from them.

Listen, look and breathe

Stop and notice what is around you. Where are you? What can you hear? What can you smell? While I write, I can hear rainbow lorikeets and spring rain outside my window. As the rain pelts down on my tin roof I am immediately struck with a strong sense of gratitude for the comfort of my home. I am protected from the harshness of nature and at this very moment I am happy. Now take slow and mindful breaths, which will help you to absorb your surroundings and allow you to utilise your senses and appreciate what you do have in your life, right now, right in front of you. Take a moment to listen, look and breathe. What are you overcome by? Sometimes the simple sensation of air filling into your chest is something really quite miraculous. You are alive.

Do something small for another who needs help

Sometimes we meet another in life who is less fortunate than us. Sometimes it is a human, sometimes it is a dog. But those who are in need can reciprocate with a gift far greater than the help you provide to them. They can provide the gift of gratitude. By doing a charitable act, we are reminded of the things that we take for granted in life, be it food, warmth or shelter.

Each year, hundreds of thousands of dogs die in shelters, deprived of the freedoms they are entitled to. They experience pain, hunger, fear and cold. They are robbed of joy and comfort and end their lives alone and unloved. Knowing this, how could we ever feel ungrateful? Our own dogs are a constant reminder of the privileges so many others never experience. Your commitment to your dog, your responsibility for their care and your reciprocated love means one less dog dies from neglect and carelessness. For that we should all be grateful.

Write it down

I have a little blackboard on my coffee table that says 'be grateful'. I wrote it months ago and its mere presence is a strong reminder for me to consider and acknowledge the good in that moment. Sometimes we need to remind ourselves that there is good around us. Often we need to be prodded a little to think about it. Writing it down can help you to visualise your gratitude. I try to write down two to three things I am grateful for each day. Sometimes they are simple things such as, 'I am grateful for the warmth of my bed.' Or, 'I am grateful for the first drops of rain on a dry and beaten ground.' If we look, we can find endless beauty and satisfaction with what we have in our lives. Even in times of great loss and pain, life presents us with a glimmer of opportunity; we just need the courage to look for it. There is always good if we focus on it.

CASE STUDY

Hogan was a sweet wiry terrier, whose owner John had bought him from a pet shop for his teenage daughter Emily. The pet shop was a commercial company that displayed Hogan and his siblings in a glass pen, only big enough for them to turn around and lie down. Being on display for hours on end, Hogan and the other puppies spent much of their time sleeping and attempting to play, but the confines of the enclosure were not especially conducive to natural puppy behaviours. John chose Hogan because he was the quietest puppy and looked the best behaved. John didn't know what he'd gotten himself into.

Whilst Emily was overwhelmed with gratitude for this puppy's arrival, John and Hogan did not get off to a very good start. Hogan had explored John's shoes from the inside out with his teeth, and discovered what the couch cushions were made of, displaying them from one end of the lounge room to the other. Hogan also piddled on John's lap during the rare times John showed interest in Hogan.

I received a phone call the next day. John called me for help with this seemingly insolent dog. He told me that if I didn't visit the next day, he would take Hogan back to the pet shop when his daughter was at school for a 'full refund'. I reluctantly accepted his threat and knocked on the door some twelve hours later.

Hogan was a glorious little puppy. There was nothing wrong with him, he just had no direction or boundaries. It was like putting a three–year-old child in a room with food and water and telling them to fend for themselves. Hogan was being set up to fail. And he was.

I showed John and Emily how to set Hogan up for success. Whilst John grumbled and stumbled, Emily was a natural.

Emily taught Hogan:

- *To go outside every hour and when he toileted, he was praised and showered with treats*
- *That there were toys he could chew and play with and that the couch was a place of rest and relaxation*
- *That sitting got him what he wanted*
- *That jumping up, excitable or testing behaviours never resulted in much worth his time*

Emily understood Hogan. But John was still prepared to give him up if need be. Such a grumpy sod John was! I didn't hear from them for years after that day and I often wondered what happened to the wiry little terrier.

John, Emily and Hogan lived in a private and magnificent part of bushland territory. It was the sort of place you'd visit to get away from everything. Lush forests, full of life and diversity. It was like entering a different world and I could see that whilst bushlands fall risk to natural disasters, the inclusive community and magnificent environment outweighed any threat from Mother Nature. For as long as Hogan was with them, he would have a lovely life there.

But whilst Mother Nature lovingly adorned their home with fresh air, ancient gums and wildlife, she had a devastating plan up her sleeve. There had been a series of unbearably hot days with unrelenting threats of bushfires. And just like that, the threats became real. It was one of the worst fires anyone had seen in Australia. A catastrophic event that will remain in the hearts of us all, but particularly the hundreds of people who were there and whose homes were lost, stock burnt and families destroyed.

Emily and Hogan were home when the fires struck. John was away for work and although he knew of the extreme fire warnings, their town hadn't been deemed officially under threat. Emily had assured her father that she was fine and that she would leave with Hogan immediately if they were in any danger. Neither of them could have predicted how quickly the fires would come or how powerful they would be. And on that devastating day, Emily lost her life. She was found outside her home the next day. Hogan was found later, left behind at what was left of their house.

By some miracle, Hogan had survived. John told me what had happened only last year. I was traveling for work and ran into him in the town where he had lost everything some years before. He was broken still and I wouldn't have expected anything different after losing his only child. But something else was different. We had a coffee and he opened up to me after half an hour of idle social niceties. I listened with respect and empathy, hanging on his every word. He told me how hard the first year was. His home was gone, his daughter was gone. There was only one thing that kept him going. I wasn't sure what he meant until he looked under the table we were sitting at, and smiled. It was Hogan.

Hogan was an old chap, still sporting the puppy eyes I remembered from years ago, but in a much older body. So was John. John told me how Hogan saved him. This dog was the only thing left that connected him to Emily. Hogan had become his lifeline. He would force John out of bed each morning, sit beside him as he cried and lay with him as he slept. He had become his confidant and his best friend. John looked at Hogan with so much love that day and then he told me something I will never forget.

After everything he had lost, John told me that Hogan taught him how to be grateful.

Hogan had become John's daily reminder to appreciate

life's little moments. That every day presents an opportunity and life should never be taken for granted. Whilst John will remain a broken soul in many ways, that faithful dog at his side had given him the chance to rebuild what little he had left.

This story is a reminder for me too. It got me to thinking about what I am grateful for. And each time I think of it, nothing material ever makes the list.

I think about John's story and the countless others who have suffered terrible tragedies. Even thinking about Hogan's life in the pet shop as a puppy. How might his life have begun in a puppy farm?

Sadly, although every dog I meet is inherently an embodiment of gratitude, many dogs in our care don't receive what they need; the basic comforts essential to survival and happiness, particularly in breeding facilities. Animal welfare continues to be overlooked on the agenda of many in power, with very little interest in understanding what animals actually need and what they truly deserve.

THE FIVE FREEDOMS

Over the past few decades, we have come to realise more and more that the welfare of animals in our care requires a consistent policy. The 'five freedoms' policy outlines the key aspects of animal welfare under human control. Drafted originally in the sixties as a response to the questionable treatment of livestock in the UK, it is now a widespread policy implemented by organisations across the world. Simplistic in its mandate, it serves as an essential guide to animals' most basic needs.

Based on the RSPCA's animal welfare framework, I have included below the five basic rights all animals should have when under the control of humans. The RSPCA also stipulates that these freedoms are best provided if those involved with livestock are caring, responsible, skilled, knowledgeable, considerate and humane.

1. **Freedom from hunger or thirst** by way of ready access to fresh water and a diet to maintain full health and vigour.
2. **Freedom from discomfort** by providing an appropriate environment including shelter and a comfortable resting area.
3. **Freedom from pain, injury or disease** by prevention or rapid diagnosis and treatment.
4. **Freedom to express (most) normal behaviour** by providing sufficient space, proper facilities and company of the animal's own kind.
5. **Freedom from fear and distress** by ensuring conditions and treatment which avoid mental suffering.

Of course, a policy is put in place with the belief it will be consistently implemented. Sometimes the five freedoms policy is, sometimes it isn't. To me, the policy is a good start, but it doesn't go far enough. What I want is a compulsory education system where empathy is an essential learning tool for all students, and respect for all living things is embedded into the minds of children. I want to see ill treatment of animals observed as a behavioural indicator of poor mental health and a psychological precursor to violence. We know there is a correlation between people who treat animals with cruelty and generalised violence. I can see opportunity for great change in political and belief systems. How someone treats an animal is a reflection of their character.

CAN DISCOMFORT BE A GOOD THING?

Some experts say that we need to be faced with the stressors of life in order for us to be grateful. If we are continuously free from all pain, distress, discomfort and hunger, what have we got to strive toward? If we are exposed to discomfort, we are grateful for its absence. If we are faced with hunger, we are grateful for food. This got me to thinking about our dogs. Perhaps the reason for the simplicity of their gratitude is because their access to basic rights is less predictable than it is for us. They help remind us to be thankful of the fundament things in life.

When we experience relief from any discomfort or deprivation, we should acknowledge it. The simplicity of acknowledging the five freedoms in our own lives may be the Sangraal to true contentedness and genuine happiness.

So what are some of the things your dog might be intrinsically grateful for? Here are just some examples:

- Warmth in their bed
- Access to safety
- Good food
- Fresh water
- Shelter
- Companionship of their own kind
- Companionship of an animal of another species
- General comfort
- Health
- Being free of pain and injury
- Space to play, run and stretch their legs
- Opportunities to explore and discover
- Being able to move away from what frightens them
- Making choices they feel are in their best interests

These essential freedoms provide your dog with genuine fulfilment.

But what about our human freedoms? What is it that we want compared to what we need? There is no respectable psychological study on earth that suggests having everything we want makes us happy, or that acquiring materials is the key to genuine happiness and fulfilment. If we channel our inner gratitude and allow our dogs to guide the way, we will see the world through a whole new lens. A grateful life has more colour in it. You hear the birds sing and you smell the freshly cut grass. You spend time outdoors playing with your dog instead of reprimanding them, and your relationships improve. An existence filled with gratitude will result in a happier, healthier and longer life.

Did you know . . . *even Plato incorporated dogs into his teachings, saying that 'a dog has the soul of a philosopher'?*

13.
Mindfulness

Over the past decade or so the ancient religious practice of mindfulness has been stripped of its spiritual connotations and modernised into a pop culture zeitgeist that people all over the world are signing up to.

Psychology, self-help books, corporate conferences, how-to DVDs and colouring books have made their way into our world with the promise that if we slow down and take the time to live in the moment, we will all be better off. But where did it all begin?

Essential to Buddhist practice is what's called 'sati'. The first of seven factors to enlightenment, sati is the faculty of mindfulness and awareness. At its core is the need to become aware of our place on the earth and to acknowledge that there are a multitude of feelings involved in that experience. In any moment there is darkness and light, with an accompanying range of feelings to be experienced and accepted.

Incorporating the teachings and doctrines of the Buddha, 'dharma' is another concept of central importance in Eastern philosophy and religion. Despite countless attempts to translate its meaning for the Western world, the closest interpretation is 'the right way of living'. With its rich tapestry of meanings across time, in certain contexts it provides guidance for people to behave in ways that are necessary for order within the universe, nature, family and oneself. It is a doctrine to avoid chaos by accepting the constancy of change.

This got me to thinking again about having compassion, self-control and a strong sense of justice (cognitive empathy). If we were to live on this earth under the guidance of these virtues, we would be better off. So would our dogs.

The spirit of a person, their internal state, their beliefs and their very existence affects their dog. Often it is the chaos in our lives and the unrelenting attempts to change what we cannot that has the biggest impact on us and those around us. We seem to be caught between the pull of cognitive empathy against emotional empathy, lured into the chaos and anxiety of life's pressures (emotional empathy) while attempting to control our own impulses and compassion (cognitive empathy). Unfortunately, most of the time, chaos dominates and we find ourselves falling into its deep and seemingly inescapable trap. But why?

Emotional empathy can be chaotic. It seems to be where we lose self-control, and are overcome with a sense of compassion and justice, leaving us caught up in a trap of emotional disorder. This is exactly what Buddhism tries to avoid. This is exactly what your dog wants you to avoid.

When I talk about capturing the good – as described in Chapter 5 – I am asking you in many ways to adopt the philosophy of mindfulness and embrace aspects of Buddhism that enable you to reward the 3 Cs: *calm, cooperative* and *controlled* behaviours and mindsets. When we reinforce these, we are, in essence, avoiding chaos. We are behaving in ways that are necessary for order within the universe, nature, our families, ourselves and our dogs. We are beginning to practise the ancient form of mindfulness.

While I do believe that practising – and reinforcing others' – calm, cooperative and controlled behaviours makes us happier, mindfulness is not about finding happiness. It is about inspiring us to change our perception of the world and our place within it, and to remain unmoved among life's inevitable changes.

Studies suggest that when practised correctly, mindfulness can reduce the symptoms of stress and increase positive emotions. Under fMRI scans, the amygdala (the part of the mid brain that reacts to stress) has been observed to reduce in size after subjects practised a modern form of mindfulness. We might say that the emotional brain became more a more cognitive brain. In addition, it was found that many participants were able to tolerate pain better. Even though pain receptors in the brain were more active, the subjects reported experiencing less pain when practising mindfulness.

CASE STUDY

Bruce, Judy and I crossed paths at a time when they were both struggling with chronic and severe anxiety. Bruce was a mastiff and Judy was his loving but equally neurotic owner. Judy contacted me via email and it was the longest explanation of canine anxiety I had ever come across. A thesis if you like. It was over 3000 words long.

Judy was a nurse in a busy emergency department, who worked a series of strange hours combining night and day shifts each week. Bruce's routine was non-existent and, as a result, both were suffering severely. Bruce had eaten the couch, the doors, the chairs, the washing machine and the dryer. He had attacked the neighbouring dogs on both sides of the house and across the road. He even terrorised each person who walked by, running repeatedly up and down the boundary fence, snapping through the gaps of timber that separated him from his victims. Bruce had become a serious liability.

I had been called by the local shelter regarding this 'dangerous' dog who was about to be surrendered by Judy. Many shelters are understandably reluctant to accept dogs like Bruce, not just because of the danger to volunteers and other dogs but because of the potential risk they posed if adopted out into society. Usually, these dogs are euthanised. I always want to know what I am dealing with however, and so I was given permission to contact Judy before she had surrendered him. Judy agreed to meet me and introduce me to her modern day Cujo.

I will never forget this dog. It was one of the few times in which I wondered what I was getting myself into. His face was a combination of exhausted and angry. His mouth oozed with saliva and I wasn't sure if it was because he had a taste for me as his next victim or if he was finishing off his last. He barked and lunged at me before I got through the front gate and I stood there. I stood with my side towards him and knelt down so we were at the same level. Bruce stopped barking.

He walked over to me behind the gate and took the food I had thrown in to him like a lion in a cage. Judy ran outside toward me, humiliated and apologetic. Her head was covered in a towel and she was brushing her teeth. She apologised profusely and proceeded to tell me that she hadn't seen Bruce like this since she started full time work at the hospital. I smiled and calmly opened the gate, whilst Judy held Bruce back. Immediately, I felt Bruce's oversized muzzle pry open my hands and fish out the remains of the treats I had brought with me.

Bruce trotted alongside me, occasionally hesitant of my presence but mostly willing to welcome me into his home, and so I obliged. Judy finished brushing her teeth, talking to me whilst she spat out the toothpaste and brushed her hair. She sat down beside us and began reciting the exhaustive email she had written only days before. I listened and let her finish what she needed to say.

When the story had finished and Bruce was asleep, I asked Judy how she was feeling. Judy began to cry and Bruce proceeded to wake up and sit beside her. The worst of her cries sent Bruce into a frenzy, as he ran and latched with full force on to my arm. The only thing separating us was my thick bomber jacket, of which the stuffing bore most of the brunt. Bruce's body mass pulled me down to my knees as he stood there pulling against my arm in deathly silence. I sat with him and let him calm down, hoping his jaws wouldn't preference anything closer to my head or neck. And whilst I could feel my arm had made contact with his teeth, there was no pain. He let go after what seemed an eternity and began barking at me, overcome with anxiety and confusion. Judy was overcome with terror and began crying more than before. I begged her to stop, hoping she would see that her anxiety caused Bruce to redirect on to me. When she squealed, Bruce would bite me. Finally she stopped, and so did Bruce. I was never afraid of Bruce. I was more concerned about his welfare with his owner. After I had made good use of the first aid kit's bandages and we had all regrouped, Judy began to talk about her life, her past, her present and her work. She had a very stressful job, and was suffering from chronic anxiety. I must have been the first person who sat with her and didn't interrupt her and soon she began to hear herself talk. She stopped and looked up at me. At this point, Bruce had begun panting and pacing around her and Judy's eyes opened wide with a revelation.

Judy had realised that Bruce was a reflection of her. His destructive behaviours occurred when she worked different shifts, where he suffered separation anxiety. His aggression toward the neighbouring dogs was his desperate attempt to control and protect his boundaries. His incessant barking at passers by was the futile need to feel safe. He was just as much a mess as she was. She had created this mess and now she had to clean it up.

I asked Judy to put Bruce on-lead, pick up his bed and find somewhere quiet. I followed her to the back verandah, where she sat with Bruce under an old oak that had been there at least fifty years before we planted ourselves beside it. Judy taught Bruce to go to his bed and lie there beside her. I asked Judy just to focus on her breathing, with her hand on Bruce's chest as he lay uncertain of her changed mood and behaviour. She closed her eyes, took in deep breaths and upon each exhalation, I saw Bruce's body relax. Only a minute had gone by before both dog and owner were in sync. Their bodies relaxed, their minds cleared, their breath slowed and steadied. They were *calm*. They were *cooperating*. They were *controlled*.

I quietly walked away and let Judy just be in the moment with her dog. Nobody to answer to, no pressure, no deadlines, just two animals becoming one. I left Judy's home knowing that she and Bruce would be there together a while, and they were. Judy called me an hour later apologising for sitting with her dog outside for so long. I laughed and told her that it was exactly what she was supposed to do. She told me that Bruce was still in his bed asleep and that she hadn't seen him so relaxed in a long time. In fact, she hadn't been so relaxed in a long time either.

Judy had come a long way, but I reminded her that she

would need to be proactive, perhaps see a psychologist to learn how to apply mindfulness to her life regularly and that the only way Bruce would change would be if she did first. I spoke with her two weeks after our breakthrough and she had relapsed. Life had gone back to the way it was. Bruce was suffering separation anxiety just like before, her night shifts were into their eighth day and she had just lost her new couch to Bruce's frustration.

It was disappointing to hear, but not a surprise. Changing your choices, your mind and your life takes time, even a failure here and there. I told Judy that failure was part of the journey. The ebbs and flows toward success require one's mastery of CPR. Judy acknowledged that she needed more *consistency*, *patience* and *respect* towards Bruce and also towards herself. I became a large contributor of support to Judy over a period of six months. She took two steps forward, then regressed backward a steps, over and over, until one day she took two steps forward and stood there. Judy had reached a point in her life in which her daily mindfulness exercises with Bruce had taken effect. She had been offered another job that had regular daily working hours and began training Bruce at her local obedience club.

Bruce's destructive behaviours disappeared. His anxiety plummeted and their relationship became one based on mutual trust and respect. Judy and Bruce now live in a different state, Judy has a different job and even runs her own yoga classes, with dogs! Just when you think your life can't change, that your unhelpful thinking habits are ingrained and that you have failed too many times, think of Judy and Bruce. Courage, persistence and desire became part of Judy's character. And whilst she could have given up and continued life as it had always been, she knew she deserved better, that Bruce deserved better. Finally, they both got what the deserved.

MINDFULNESS THROUGH DOGNITIVE THERAPY

Know what you can control and what you cannot

Think back to the mantra, 'Give me the serenity to accept the things I cannot change, the courage to change the things I can and the wisdom to know the difference.'

In Chapter 6 we talked about controllability and predictability. Our survival depends on feeling in control and being able to predict our environment. But we can't always achieve this. Ultimately, nothing is truly in our control.

While we exist on this earth within a comparatively tiny solar system among the infinite universe, we are reminded of our insignificance. Within this realisation, there is a sense of calm. The pressure of life is removed from our tired shoulders and we can appreciate that every moment we are alive is a moment not to be taken for granted.

Try to be cognitively empathic

In Chapter 5 we looked into the differences between cognitive empathy and emotional empathy. Being able to consciously distance our compassion for others helps us avoid falling into the traps of an emotional chaos. It is easier said than done with our loved ones, I know, and I am not about to ask anyone to emotionally remove themselves from those closest to them. But I do want you to adopt an approach that gives you the strength to think more rationally, to find self-control and, where possible, to see everything in your world as one.

Capture every moment that is good

In Chapter 7 we discussed the importance of seizing the good moments around us. There are probably hundreds of moments in every day that are good. How many you find is relative to how willing you are to look.

From smelling the fresh air outside to savouring that lingering taste of melted chocolate in your mouth, there is good all around us. But capturing the good is not just about sensory pleasures, it is also about looking for the good in others. Those in your life offer you selflessness, kindness and good all the time. Your dogs are a great example of this. If you look, you will see your dog displaying countless behaviours that are conducive to a respectful and trusting relationship.

Reward the calm, cooperative and controlled behaviours and mindsets of yourself and those around you

As we've touched on throughout this book, the 3 Cs are an overarching approach to dognitive therapy. They are the things we look for in others around us, particularly those who depend on our guidance, including our dogs and children. But they are also the mindsets and behaviours we want to reward within ourselves. For our dogs, the 3 Cs are the things we want to focus on rewarding.

They are also essential to incorporate into our own practice of mindfulness. They help promote a healthy mind, a positive outlook and happy and healthy relationships with those around us.

Trust and respect yourself

In Chapter 4 we discussed the importance of trust and respect – not just that of others, but our own too. We cannot engage in positive relationships with anyone until we find trust and respect within our own mind and body. You know yourself better that any other and at some point in your life you have to prove that. Stop comparing yourself to everything that is out of your control. When we believe in ourselves and feel comfortable in our own skin, others' perception of us becomes immaterial.

Dogs are our best teachers. They are a reflection of our own internal state. If we don't respect and trust ourselves, they won't either.

Be grateful

In the previous chapter you will have become well acquainted with the benefits of gratitude. In so many moments, there is an opportunity to be grateful.

When external influences overwhelm you, which they undoubtedly will from time to time, stop. Stop your body, slow your mind and steady your emotions. Can you control the events? If you can't, accept that you can't and focus on the good in that moment. Don't get caught up in the chaos, and instead be rational and trust yourself enough to follow your own judgement. Be kind whenever possible and look for the good in others. Never be afraid to reach out and say thank you when someone cooperates with you, and acknowledge those who are calm and controlled. Be grateful. You may not have everything you want, but right in front of you is everything you need.

Learn from your dog. Watch them and study their movements. Let them teach you about mindfulness. Let them show you how to appreciate simplicities and necessities. Allow them to encourage you to make the most of every moment, appreciating what you do have rather than grieving for what you don't.

Your dog is your reflection and in many ways your guide. They will tell you who you are, but they will also show you who you could be. They will open the doors to self-improvement, trust and respectful inspiration. Your dog is your key to enlightenment.

Did you know . . . *with anxiety increasingly becoming an epidemic for dogs as well as humans, the amount of anti-depressant medications prescribed for dogs is now in the millions? In 2012, it was reported that in America alone, an estimated three million owners medicated their dogs for anxiety. That's around one in ten dogs, which is the same ratio as for humans on similar medications.*

14.
The Emotions We Are Afraid Of

What is it about the modern mind that is so complicated? It really is that black box, a mystery that no matter how much we learn, we still don't know that much about. But research is slowly but surely uncovering the mysteries of the mind, revealing fascinating information.

I recently read an article published in 2003 that included fascinating input by experimental psychologist Steven Pinker. He explained: 'When a surgeon sends an electrical current into the brain, the person can have a vivid, lifelike experience.'

Pinker goes on to say that 'Every emotion and thought gives off physical signals, and the new technologies for detecting them are so accurate that they can literally read a person's mind and tell a cognitive neuroscientist whether the person is imagining a face or a place.' It seems that reading someone's mind is no longer a specialty of psychics or fantasy. Now, it's a science.

Our very existence is determined by the mind. If we do

not have our mind, we do not live. This got me to thinking once again about our emotions and perception of ourselves in this world. In 1970, the psychologist Gordon G Gallup Jr developed a test to explore self-awareness in animals. The findings brought about an acceptance that there may be a range of species outside of our own that are as aware as we are. The research suggested that chimpanzees, killer whales, elephants, dolphins and magpies displayed behaviours consistent with his test for self-awareness. However, dogs didn't seem to pass the test, which involved recognising their reflection in a mirror.

Of all the senses, a dog's vision falls well behind their sense of smell and hearing. It was and is a survival advantage to be able to smell and hear a potential mate, competitor or food source. So perhaps its not that a dog doesn't have the cognitive ability to understand a reflection, but the lack of visual ability to recognise themselves in the first place. Additionally, critics of the research believe that because of the range of different adaptions animals have, there may have been false negative results (i.e. there may be many animals that have self-awareness that can't be tested via the methods in the study).

As I sit in my study, both my dogs lie on the couch, asleep and keeping each other warm. Chester is fairly apathetic towards Alma, but Alma is quite taken with him. He is her guide. Wherever he goes she follows. As they lie there in a state of semi-consciousness, I see Chester's paws start to spasm and his upper lip begin to twitch. His third eyelid becomes visible as his eyes roll back out of view and he leaves the world to fall deep into an unconscious state.

He begins to dream, probably about his day. Perhaps the walk we went on, the splashing about in the dam, maybe even the bits of roast chicken he was snuck under the table.

Research tells us that dogs most likely do dream about their daily experiences, including their fears, joys and moments of exploration and discovery. Their emotions are collected and relived in the unconscious and it makes me wonder about how much influence their emotions have on their existence.

Fear

Fear is a response to a stimulus that can make us go into a fight, flight or freeze mode. A range of areas of the brain become active when we are fearful and decisions are made based on an immediate assessment of the threat. The stimulus is something we have been conditioned to be afraid of through past experiences or external influences. Things like spiders, speaking in public and illness are among the many things we may fear, partly because we can predict the consequences of having to encounter them but we feel we have no control over them.

For dogs, stimuli that may elicit fear can include things such as vet clinics, loud noises, the hose or a newspaper being lifted towards them. Sometimes they will run from it, other times they will freeze, but on occasion they will bite.

This saddens me from an animal-welfare perspective. If an animal is genuinely fearful and bites, is it really their fault? There is certainly some accountability on the dog's end, but it is unlikely they are consciously motivated to cause harm. They may have a poor bite inhibition, having learnt this from the owners who raised them. They may be more inclined to bite instead of flight because their own parents did. A complicated collection of factors influence a behaviour such as biting, but as the guardians of dogs, owners are the ones who should effectively manage it. Sadly, when managed poorly, the ones who suffer the most are our dogs.

Anxiety

Anxiety is different to fear. Generally, we feel anxious in a situation that is unpredictable. We may not have had a prior experience of it, we may or may not have control, but we have no real idea of what to expect. Anxiety can be experienced in a range of different situations, from a wedding day to waiting for a medical diagnosis. It can be caused by situations that you look forward to and those that you may dread. It is a complicated emotion and one that has travelled with us along the evolutionary path. Some anxiety is healthy and essential to survival. But when it begins to affect your everyday life, it can become debilitating.

For dogs, anxiety is the most common cause of unwanted behaviours. Almost invariably, when I consult with a client about their dog, the pet's behaviour is attributable to anxiety. Why is it so prevalent in dogs? And why do more and more people present with this ailment, which affects the lives of many millions across the world? The truth is, no one really knows.

A combination of genetics and the environment influence our responses to the world. Some of us manage anxiety better than others, in part because we were born with the ability to do so. Some of us retrain our thinking habits through CBT, ACT and mindfulness. Unfortunately, many never attempt to manage their negative thinking habits. Dogs too can unnecessarily endure a life of distress without a leader to recognise and manage it.

As we learn more about the brain and its interconnected complexity, we better understand the biological causes of anxiety and depression. When a nerve cell (neuron) in the brain communicates with others around it, chemical transmissions pass on messages, enabling our mind and body to function in every aspect. The chemicals that enable this are called neurotransmitters.

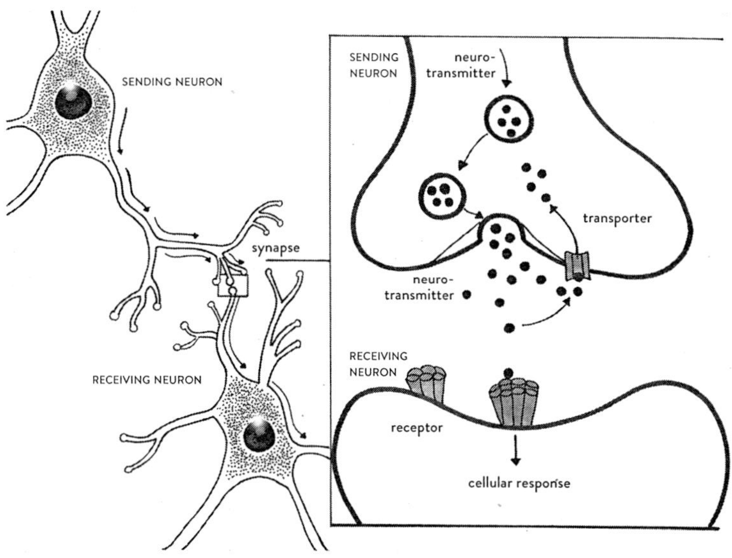

There are a number of neurotransmitters in our brain cells including GABA, endorphins, dopamine and oxytocin. But the one of most interest in anxiety disorders is serotonin.

You will see from the diagram that once serotonin has transmitted signals across the synapse (the gap between the neurons), it is then reabsorbed by the cell it is transmitting from. For animals and humans with mental illness, we now understand that serotonin is reabsorbed by the nerve cells faster than it is released into the synapse. This affects mood, appetite, social behaviour, sleep and memory, to name but a few things. In combination with CBT, ACT and mindfulness, medications called selective serotonin reuptake inhibitors (SSRIs) can assist by reducing the absorption of serotonin in the presynaptic cell (the cell the message is coming from), increasing the amount of serotonin in the synapse and reducing the symptoms of anxiety and depression.

It was thought that this was the only way that SSRIs work, but something didn't make sense. SSRIs increase the serotonin in the synapse within days of starting the medication, but it can take up to two months to have an observable affect in human patients and dogs (who can also be administered it). Something else must be going on.

Current state-of-the-art research suggests it is not just the extra serotonin in the synapse that is effective in treatment, but that this extra serotonin encourages increased production of protective nerve cell proteins like brain-derived neurotropic factor (BDNF). It just goes to show that we are constantly investigating and changing our thinking about the best ways to improve our thoughts, behaviours and lives. What will medication look like in ten years?

I am not telling you to make a visit to your doctor or vet and request a prescription for SSRIs. I just want you to see that sometimes mental health can be complicated with physiological shortfallings. By learning more about the science behind mental health and medications, we can help reduce the stigma around them.

Aggression

This word is used as much as 'dominance' in the field of dog behaviour, and both words are often misinterpreted.

Aggressive behaviours are elicited by emotions such as anger, hostility and antipathy. For some, being overcome with these can lead to violence with the intent to inflict harm on another. Most dogs are not aggressive. Even most dogs who growl, snap or bite are not inherently aggressive. So why does it present itself in countless conversations across the animal-training world?

Many argue that the evolution of aggression goes back to a primitive need to inflict harm on prey. To be able to follow through with a kill, an animal needs to experience intense and violent emotions, which makes aggression a very favourable behaviour during a hunt. But given that domesticated dogs don't need to hunt, are they simply displaying a hardwired survival technique when they display aggression, or are they somehow 'bad'?

I do still fall for the 'appeal to nature' argument, which proposes that animals are inherently good and that their behaviours are invariably determined by how they are treated. Maybe it is true, but to study this is near impossible. There are so many factors that influence our behaviour, and pinpointing a cause requires rigorous longitudinal studies.

Having said this, I do believe that my dog Chester would have been a very different dog if he were not raised in a supportive environment based on dognitive therapy. I see a very different side to him when we visit my friend's house. Under her influence, he shows some anxiety and reactivity towards the other dogs because he has no guidance on how to safely behave under her control. His drive to hunt prey skyrockets as other dogs around him chase and catch the occasional rabbit and his general emotional state sometimes goes beyond my recognition of him. But with me, Chester is a deep thinker and a sensitive soul who has exquisite impulse control, along with great trust and respect for me. I do feel very blessed, and I think he probably feels the same.

Stress reactivity

When a dog growls, snaps or bites, usually it is a reaction to a perceived threat. Sometimes the response is warranted, other times it is an overreaction. I cannot stress to you enough how taxing this world can be for your dog. There is so much thrust upon them each and every day, most of it unpredictable and uncontrollable, leaving them with a collection of emotions including anxiety, frustration and even depression. No wonder dogs are hyperreactive. But this sort of stress reactivity can have a negative impact not only on a dog's mental health, but their physical health too.

Chronic (long-term) stress in people can affect their health in many ways, from muscular-tension headaches, to obesity and even heart disease and stroke. Without management, chronic stress can reduce your life expectancy. I believe it is the same for dogs, probably worse, for their attempts to communicate their emotions and ailments are often ignored or misunderstood.

When we feel threatened, our brain prepares us for a fight, flight or freeze response. The blood from our brain is redirected to the muscles and we gain the ability to physically protect ourselves from harm. Sadly, when we are in a reactive state, we are not rational. We are unable to think logically and we may end up behaving in ways that are out of character. Sometimes dog owners will tell me that their dog is generally so well behaved and loving at home, but becomes an uncontrollable demon when taken on a walk. Often dogs who have been exposed to threatening situations in their past will have a low threshold to threats in the world and are more likely to be stress reactive. It is yet another cause of concern when it comes to animal welfare.

How can you help your dog overcome this stress?

By using CPR and reinforcing the 3 Cs, you can empower your dog over time to gain confidence and tolerance for their ever-changing world. Using desensitisation techniques and applying dognitive therapy not only allows you to encourage your dog to learn healthy strategies to deal with stress, but it builds a stronger bond based on mutual trust and respect.

Firstly, recognise your dog's threshold (the level of the stimulus they can comfortably tolerate). This could be distance, noise or speed of movement. It is important that you never overstep this point. Always try to stay at or below that point, as your goal is to empower your dog to learn helpful thinking strategies, not reinforce their fear or anxiety.

When you dog is showing any or all of the 3 Cs, they are expressing a positive affective state and at this point, you are able to consider increasing the threshold.

There will be highs and lows during this training, because you are reshaping a deep-seeded emotional state. Having empathy for your dog and setting them up for success is so important during times of learning, particularly when dealing with changing associations of perceived threats.

Phobias

It is normal to experience fear. There is a big wild world out there filled with threatening stimuli, but when our fear deprives us of healthy functioning, it takes form as a phobia. Those affected by phobias will go out of their way to avoid being faced with what it is they fear. They will spend a huge amount of time worrying about it, wondering where it is or when it might confront them.

I think of Sarah from Chapter 4, 'Trust and Respect'. Remember the fear she experienced of those dogs that barked down the street? How her daily routine and her social and working life were completely upturned from her constant worrying, avoidance and irrational thinking? Sarah had a phobia named cynophobia (a fear of dogs).

Phobias are actually quite common, with at least two million Australians suffering from one. They can be of just about anything you can imagine. Some intriguing examples include pogonophobia (beards), clinophobia (beds), paedophobia (children), nephophobia (clouds), ailurophobia (cats), cibophobia (food) and hypegiaphobia (responsibility). A lot of my clients initially present with that last one.

Our understanding of the causes of phobias remains limited, although we do know that there is a combination of genetics and environment at play. For me, as an animal behaviourist, I think about the genetics of dog breeding and wonder how many breeders are out there who prioritise the matching of two dogs based on sound and tolerant temperaments. Those who are dedicated and completely responsible most likely do. But I think there are a lot out there who don't.

When it comes to environmental influences, the fear is created and reinforced upon a negative experience. Luckily for dogs and humans there are therapies that have high (but not fool-proof) success rates when applied properly.

Exposure therapy involves a technique where patients face their fears in an innocuous setting. Dog behaviourists call this process 'desensitisation'.

There are many differences between exposure therapy for humans and dogs. Therapists are able to effectively communicate to a person that a stimulus is benign, and that they are safe and that the world won't end if exposed to it. With dogs, of course, this can't be verbally communicated, so we must be hyperaware of how a dog's subtle behaviours reflect their state of mind when they come face to face with what they fear. Timing is of utmost importance, as is the threshold of exposure. If we push a dog's limits, we risk further reinforcing the phobia, causing a breakdown of trust and respect. In essence, when we push a threshold too much, we set our dogs up for failure.

Canine compulsive disorder

This is a disorder I see often in dogs. From the excessive licking (kind of like compulsive hand washing) behaviour, to mounting, tail-chasing, excessive digging and barking, dogs have developed a repertoire of 'normal' behaviours that can cause severe problems if they become compulsive. Most of these base behaviours were necessary for survival a millennia or ten ago, but are no longer essential for a domesticated dog. However, dogs cannot help their overwhelming instinct to display them. For some dogs – particularly if they feel distressed – the behaviours can become destructively obsessive and repetitive.

So how can you curb these compulsions? It can be effective to put these behaviours 'on cue'. That is, to request the barking, digging or tail-chasing of the dog, followed by a cue and a reward to stop. Often dogs who display stereotypes are anxious and unsure, so by helping them overcome the behaviours you can build confidence and purpose in the dog.

ENSURING YOUR DOG HAS PURPOSE

No matter what type of problem your dog may face, it is essential that they feel genuine purpose in their life. There are a range of games you can play that not only fulfil your dog's physical exercise needs, but their mental needs as well. Dogs love to work. Similarly for humans, if we have no purpose, we can become anxious, insecure and depressed. We can also become destructive, reactive and antisocial. It is no different for dogs.

Purpose involves the mind and body, so find activities in which your dog is enthusiastically cooperating with you through thinking and moving. Here are some good examples.

Stop-stalk-fast

A game in which you cue your dog with these three words as you are going on a walk. 'Stop' at curbs and other intermitent points. 'Stalk' is moving slowly in anticipation of the big run when you say 'FAST!' Then you both run as fast as you can together, until you say 'stalk' or 'stop'. With this game, you are teaching your dog impulse control, whilst playing and cooperating.

Hide and seek

Teach your dog to find their food rather than giving it to them for free. Hide their food in the backyard or even inside the house. Let them know when they are getting closer by using the word 'warmer'. To begin teaching them this, you need to condition them by giving them a treat immediately when you say 'warmer'. Once they make the association, you can engage in this game, which really gets them thinking.

Play each day!

Play is so important for both of you. Just once a day, forget about everything in your lives and engage in 10 minutes of fun. Get your dog's favourite toys out, and as you throw the toys, throw out the rules as well. Sometimes a game with no rules is essential for your dog.

Lastly, keep the 3 Cs – *calm*, *cooperative* and *controlled* behaviours – constantly in the back of your mind. Practise CPR – being *consistent*, *patient* and *respectful* – and always think from your dog's point of view.

SUMMARY

We are an incredibly emotional species. Our emotions are crucial to communication within our social groups and help to build bonds between people. Unfortunately in a modern world, our emotions are hypersensitised and we find ourselves either overstimulated or paralysed by a range of feelings.

Try to be aware of your emotions. Acknowledge them and make decisions based not on your raw emotions, but on your analysis of them. Reflect on your feelings and process them with a logical mind. Remember your emotions are contagious. Anxiety, fears and phobias quickly latch onto those around you, especially your dog. If you're not careful, these emotions can become a parasite on your dog and leave them feeling even more helpless than those around them.

Did you know . . . *dogs can read our emotions in our facial expressions? Thought to be a combination of thousands of years of domestication as well as learning what facial movement goes with what consequence, dogs are attuned to our thoughts better than we realise. Research has tested this theory, finding that dogs respond with anxiety and uncertainty when we furrow our brows and with excitement and anticipation when we smile and soften our eyes.*

15.
Old Dogs and New Tricks

Of all the dogs surrendered to shelters each year, perhaps the most affected are the ones who are in their senior years. Whilst we may not know what life they may have had, we do know that older dogs are the most difficult to rehome. Amongst dogs with behaviour problems, illness, and even the Big Black Dog bias (where dogs are allegedly overlooked for being black), the elderly canines might not just want to eat the chopped liver, they are the chopped liver.

This got me to thinking about elderly humans and how there are similarities in both perception and treatment of animals and people who have been on this earth longer. In 2017, we see increased human life expectancies, with the average age of a woman reaching eighty-four years and a man eighty years. But whilst we may be living longer, the elderly seem to be living life much harder, falling between the cracks in our welfare system. Whilst our pets may not share in all the complexities of life that humans do, we can at the very least agree that both elderly animals and humans deserve our compassion and help.

CASE STUDY

Maxi had been in a shelter for over a year. She was a border collie, dearly loved by a man who suddenly passed away when she was seven. Because this man's death was so sudden, he had not prepared any family members to care for Maxi, and so the day after he passed, she was delivered to the local pound to live out one of two fates. She would either find another loving home or be put to sleep. Maxi didn't find a home. Many had walked past the confines of her pen, most commenting on her age, if they paused to look at her at all. Others were more drawn to the puppies further down the corridor and bypassed Maxi as she sat by the gate, tail wagging in hopeless anticipation.

I hadn't met Maxi until she had been waiting for over twelve months to find a home. I knew the family that ran the shelter and had heard about Maxi before. They kept her as family as much as they could, not having the heart to transfer her after having unsuccessfully attempted to rehome her themselves.

Clients of mine who were looking for a dog had contacted me a month prior, wanting to adopt a puppy. Their two children were old enough to understand how to care for a furry friend and after years of making false promises to their parents, they were finally responsible enough keep them. The two girls, aged six and eight were keen on a cavoodle and had been actively looking online, a little like one might do when searching for a new car. I knew that Marianne and Craig would give in to their girls, but they wanted me to help them on the journey.

I warned Marianne and Craig of the risks associated with buying a puppy online and once they had admitted the dogs for sale did not have parents available for viewing and most would not allow them to visit their property, I was able to convince the family to consider adopting a puppy instead. Whilst Marianne was more receptive to my suggestion than the others, they finally agreed to at least come with me to meet some puppies who had been surrendered where Maxi was residing.

I will never forget watching the facial expressions of the two young girls, Lily and Fran, as they walked up the path towards the building that housed all those lost souls. The orchestra of barks and howls made them both hide behind their mum and it struck me how confronting it can be for people in rescue organisations. Marianne explained to me that Lily had a learning disorder and became unnerved quite easily. Together with her sister Fran, Lily stopped in her tracks, turned around and walked back to the car, refusing to go any further. I could see where they were coming from but I didn't want a puppy to miss out on a potential forever home, so I convinced everyone except Lily to continue on with me, whilst she sat on the grass by the car.

We walked up to the shelter and met the volunteers who had been waiting for us. The puppies were on their way back from the vet, and were just around the corner from the property, so the four of us waited in the shade for their return. One minute went by, then five, then ten minutes, and Marianne was getting worried about leaving Lily on her own for so long. Following behind them, I returned to their car to make sure Lily was ok, but she was gone.

Everyone's heart sank – Lily was nowhere in sight. We searched around the car, down the driveway, through the shelter and even up to the house, but she was nowhere. Marianne cried out to her, bellowing in a panic and running towards the one place we all feared she might be; the dam.

As we ran down the hill towards the body of water, we were struck by a scene that none of us could ever have imagined. Lily was there, sitting in the grass beside the dam with Maxi beside her. Maxi's head had rested on Lily's legs as she ran her little hands through the greying Collie's hair, telling stories of her first day at school. The family had found the dog they were searching for. Their perfect new puppy was old Maxi.

Lily told us that Maxi had followed her down to the dam and as Lily reached down to play near the water, Maxi barked for her attention. Lily thought Maxi was telling her something so she followed her back to the bank of the dam and sat with her under the willow tree that shaded them both from the harsh country sun.

It was one of those moments where I knew everyone there was thinking what I already knew. They were in awe of this dog. This dog was someone who would look after them, glue them and love them. They would do the same for her. And they did. Maxi was eight years old. Marianne and Craig worried that being her age, the girls might be facing heartbreak in the near future. But that was seven years ago.

Maxi is fifteen now, still sitting beside the girls as they do their homework with their friends in the lounge and gossip about boys. She sleeps at the end of Lily's bed each night. And whilst Lily is now fifteen too, any time she feels nervous or unsure of what the world has in store for her, Maxi is always right by her side.

Lily has taught Maxi many new tricks. Maxi knows over fifty words, including, teddy, bear, dolly and chicken. According to the girls, these are Maxi's favourite toys. Marianne told me that ever since Maxi entered their lives, Lily's learning disorder reduced substantially. From having trouble communicating and socialising with others at school, she is now a School House Captain and also on the debating team. Often, Marianne catches Lily running her speeches by Maxi for initial approval before delivering them to her class or the entire school. 'Maxi has made us all better people,' says Marianne.

We tend to overlook older dogs. We tend to overlook older people too. But they both have so much to offer. Stories of wisdom, life experience, hardships and victories are all there to be told. If we listen to their stories, we open our hearts and minds to learning many of life's lessons. We learn about trust and respect. We learn about sacrifice, empathy and compassion. We learn from them there is a lot more about this life we actually don't know.

Don't let age fool you when adopting a dog. Old dogs bring with them a great deal of life experience. They are incredibly appreciative, grateful and easily contented, but their drive to learn new things and explore the world makes them ageless. You *can* teach an old dog new tricks.

Here are my favourite activities for older dogs who may have the mind of a puppy but a body slightly less agile.

Let them use their nose

Allow them to search for food and follow other smells that result in rewards. No matter the age, a dog's sense of smell is still acute and they love exploring with it.

You might use a smell such as lavender and associate it with a high-value treat. Then you can hide it, motivating them to go and find it for a reward. It is not only great for their mind, but also for your relationship together.

Teach them Target Training

Teach them to touch their nose to your hand for a reward. You can use this approach to get them to move around, even do low intensity exercise to build muscle in their hips and back legs from targeting their nose to your hand positioned beside their shoulder. Target training is great brain exercise that you can build on, plus it has been shown to improve the confidence of dogs when in uncertain situations. For example, if your dog is feeling a little unsure, cue them to target to your hand. This redirects their attention towards something positive and gives them a sense of control.

Exercise is Important

Low intensity exercise is so beneficial for older dogs. Swimming is ideal as it builds strength without impact on joints. But there are also other low impact activities your dog will enjoy. Walking is very low impact, provided it is not too far and the weather is optimal. One trick is to teach your dog to bow and give high fives, and they are great stretch exercises too. To teach your dog to bow, condition them with a clicker or word such as 'yes' to mean food is coming. Once the association of the noise has been made with yummy treats, you can capture your dog stretching when they get out of their bed and immediately say 'yes' with great enthusiasm followed by an overwhelming number of treats and praise. You can then introduce a word like 'bow' and before you know it, your dog will be bowing at your presence, like you're royalty.

Teach them to Retrieve

Although your older dog may not be able to leap up and catch a frisbee mid-air anymore, it doesn't mean that they don't want to play or retrieve for you. Your dog at their age may need purpose more than ever so teach them to find toys and bring them back to you. Many exercises that are designed for outdoors can be modified for inside. You can even teach your dog to drop the toys into a bucket or chest, or learn the names of each toy. The more active the mind, the longer it lasts.

Patients diagnosed with Alzheimer's are not always elderly. But no matter what age, there can be no doubt that it is a devastating disease affecting millions of people worldwide each year. The degeneration of the brain is what causes symptoms of the disease, including cognitive impairment, forgetfulness and behaviour out of character. The disease is complex with no known cure, although rigorous research continues on with hope for a future that can not only cure Alzheimer's, but even prevent it.

Some evidence has shown that people who have been mentally active throughout their life, or are highly educated are less likely to be diagnosed with Alzheimer's. There is speculation that patients who are highly educated and have a higher level of cognitive functioning have more mental room to move, so to speak, when it comes to reaching the lower threshold of cognitive decline. Neuroscience researchers term this as having *cognitive reserve.* This makes me think about how increasing the activity of neural pathways in humans can improve cognitive functioning. And, if it can, surely the same applies to dogs.

Like Marianne and Craig, many people are hesitant to adopt older dogs because of alleged health concerns or the thought that their new pet is on borrowed time. Whilst there are always risks that older animals will suffer from disease and may leave the earth earlier, they are still animals. They still have needs and deserve to be given a second chance. Even their reduced agility and tiring bones are cause for concern, the benefits of saving an elderly dog soon outweigh the negatives. Less attention in other areas is required, including toilet training, exercise routines and destructive behaviours.

It is so disheartening to see that senior canines are the ones left behind at pounds and shelters, all because they appear to be past their use-by date. Most shelters I have worked with have confessed that older dogs are even more difficult to adopt over dogs with medium to severe behavioural issues. It makes me think of Alma, my other dog, who came to me with a combination of physical and mental downfalls. Her ears had closed over due to untreated infections, her feet were red-raw from allergies and her behaviour towards other dogs was hyperreactive and anxious. Alma would spend hours on end repeatedly licking her paws and scratching her ears upon our initial acquaintance. She would lunge at dogs behind fences and nip at those who got a little too close for comfort.

It took time for Alma to overcome her severe and debilitating allergies. I used what had been recommended to me to no avail until one day, I discovered her paws were dry, as if they hadn't been licked at all. The next day, there were no signs of irritation either and soon a pattern formed. She finally felt safe. There was no irritation in body or mind any longer.

Whilst she will occasionally begin to lick her paws, I watch her stop all of a sudden and just relax. It is almost as if she realises there is nothing to be stressed about and she calms down immediately.

Interestingly when some dogs feel anxious or excitable, they are more likely to experience itchiness. You might see your dog scratch for no apparent reason, particularly when at the dog park, or in the car. Anxiety in people can increase the likelihood of skin irritations and the same goes for dogs.

So, if you or your dog is under stress, your body may be responding by releasing cortisol. Released from the adrenal glands, cortisol works by providing the body with glucose in preparation for a fight, flight or freeze response. One of the many trade-offs of this stress hormone can be itchiness. Have you ever seen someone scratch their arm or head when they are socially confronted? Whilst there are a range of causes for this, one suggestion is that acute stress can compromise the functioning of the body's organs. With the skin being the largest organ in the body, it is no surprise that it seems to suffer severely during times of distress.

SYMPTOMS OF STRESS

Stress can cause a range of symptoms for people including the following:

Behaviour

- Not going out anymore
- Not getting things done at work/school
- Withdrawing from close family and friends
- Relying on alcohol and sedatives
- Not doing usual enjoyable activities
- Inability to concentrate

Feelings

- Overwhelmed
- Guilty
- Irritable
- Frustrated
- Lacking in confidence
- Unhappy
- Indecisive
- Disappointed
- Miserable
- Sad

Thoughts

- 'I'm a failure.'
- 'It's my fault.'

- 'Nothing good ever happens to me.'
- 'I'm worthless.'
- 'Life's not worth living.'
- 'People would be better off without me.'

Physical

- Tired all the time
- Sick and run down
- Headaches and muscle pains
- Churning gut
- Sleep problems
- Loss or change of appetite
- Significant weight loss or gain

All cited from beyondblue.org.au

The next time you are stressed, ask yourself is it really worth it?

SUMMARY

Age does not need to have an expiration date attached to it. Adopting an older dog is a wonderful choice as they bring so much life experience with them. They are also great teachers of how important it is to keep the mind active with positive purpose. Additionally, more experienced dogs remind us to be mindful and accepting. The elderly's approach to life tends to be calm, cooperative and controlled, and whilst they may be a little slower to move, they are superior in wisdom and experience. We have a lot to learn from them.

Did you know . . . *one female dog and a litter of her female pups can produce up to 4372 puppies over seven years? This is one of many reasons to spay and neuter dogs and prevent hundreds of thousands of dogs being exposed to shelters or becoming homeless. Spayed dogs generally live longer, are less susceptible to disease and are reported to be happier.*

16.
Wellbeing and the Body

He is built for the kill. Phenomenal strength and might from nose to tail give him an extraordinary ability to run, and to stalk and pounce on unsuspecting prey. The striated muscles along his skeleton support oscillating body movements as he moves from left to right; each movement a step ahead of his victim. His ears are elongated and elevated, attuned to subtle movements in the grass ahead, and as he moves forward with great patience and steadiness, his eyes fixate on the target. He is fast, intelligent and motivated. He is ready to end the game.

As he leaps into the air, eyes and mouth widened, the prey surrenders in inevitable defeat against his dominant hunting prowess. Chester picks up the kill, shakes it in a frenzy intended to destroy each and every bone in its body. Luckily, however, this particular victim merely has a rubbery, mass-manufactured body. The purple duck we received as a Christmas present only lasted days, and although its life was short-lived compared to the lives of the real wildlife on our property, it served a very important purpose to Chester's mental and physical health. It allowed him to expend a predatory energy hardwired within him, without causing harm to another animal.

I am always amazed at my dogs' restraint when around potential prey at home. We have several species of birds on our property, from cockatoos and galahs, to Pacific black ducks, Aussie wood ducks, chestnut teals and swamp hens. They greet us each morning near the seed bin that gets our beloved birdlife through the harsh summers. My dogs clumsily plod along each side of me as the birds flock to the tree that I approach, as if they are flying into an avian airport, and accept the seeds I have in my hands. Chester and Alma are particularly interested in the offerings that fall from my hands that provide an opportunity to forage along with the ducks. I do laugh to myself as I see these Staffordshire bull terriers, historically 'bred' for their bear-maiming and dog-fighting capabilities, happily looking for leftover seed alongside vulnerable feathered prey.

Dog breeds and our careful selection of dog 'types' has resulted in over 300 different breeds, all serving some purpose to our needs. We are a demanding species! Each breed with different hair, snouts, shapes and sizes, and different abilities and purposes, all artificially created to serve us. What does that say about us?

Dogs vary in size from 6.5 cm to 250 cm in length and have a range of adaptations to meet our needs, rather than theirs. From pugs to Great Danes, we have created the only species on earth whose various breeds bear little resemblance to each other. But no matter how they look or how they have come to be in existence, dogs and their diversity continue to blow our minds. Their structural, behavioural and physiological adaptations are still reminiscent of their common ancestor, the wolf, which was and still is an impressive predatory species.

Let's take a look at the fascinating bodies of the modern dog.

Predatory mouth

A dog's mouth has a design that serves various purposes. Their mouths can open open wide, almost as if their jaw is on an elastic hinge, and upon occlusion can bite down with great force. Humans, who historically were scavengers, evolved with an ability to chew food well. But a dog snaps rather than chews, sometimes tilting its head while quickly consuming its prey, with digestion occurring further down the track, or should I say tract.

Paws

When I look at a dogs paw, the first thing I notice is the fatty pad. A shock absorber, a temperature regulator and a calloused protector from the terrain they encounter. Ever wondered why your dog's feet smell like corn chips? It's because of the sweat glands at the base of their feet. All the bacteria in between their toes mixed with a little moisture makes for an interesting scent that many find reminiscent of nachos.

Dogs are digitigrade, meaning that they walk about on their toes. In fact, if you look at an X-ray, you will see that your dog moves about on their tippy toes. Allowing for gripping the ground and running at optimal speed, the carpal bones of their paws are designed for hunting.

Humans, by contrast, are not built for speed. Our evolutionary path took us in a different direction that gave precedence to the best methods to conserve energy and having a bigger brain. Our feet are plantigrade, meaning that we walk on the entire soles of our feet. Looking at an X-ray, you would see that the bones are flat to the ground. This allowed us to stand upright many millions of years ago, meaning it took less energy to move about to focus on finding high-protein foods that arguably led to us becoming the smartest animal on the planet by nourishing our brains.

Speed

A quadruped (four-footed) animal will always run faster than a biped (two-footed). The greyhound has adaptations unlike any other dog, with their deep chests, flexible spines, slender lines and muscular legs. They top speeds of up to seventy kilometres per hour, and it is no surprise that their fast running has taken the form of sport for our entertainment.

Animals have been used for sport since the beginning of time. Such sports have become embedded into our culture. But to me, it all comes down to choice. If an animal is forced into a situation, if they are euthanised because of a performance injury and if they are objectified for profit, then what does that say about us? A greyhound is no different to a pet dog in mind and body. So even when they are rehomed upon retirement, what sort of emotional impact does that have on them? I am not heading a campaign to end all animal sports here, but I do think that the way an animal is treated is a direct reflection of who we are. I am not entirely sure the racing industry necessarily reflects favourably on those involved.

Tail

Chester's tail is one of my favourite things about him. It is so expressive and communicates to me with each movement it makes. I can tell so much about him by his tail – his fears, anxieties, disappointments and desires.

Research suggests that the direction in which the tail moves is also an indication of the dog's emotional state. When a tail is wagging more to the right it suggests the dog is feeling positive, while wagging to the left can suggest quite the opposite.

Neuroscientists from the University of Trieste in Italy, along with veterinarians, described this revelation in *Current Biology*. They placed thirty pet dogs of various breeds into separate enclosures with cameras that could track the movement of their tails. All dogs were exposed to four different stimuli separately, including their owner, an unknown person, a cat and an unknown 'dominant' dog. Can you guess what happened when the dog saw their owner? You're correct. Their tails wagged furiously with a right-wagging bias. Interestingly, when they saw an unfamiliar person, they still wagged with a right-side bias, but less so. When the dogs saw the cat, researchers found that their tails still wagged more to the right, though it was more reserved and slow. With exposure to unfamiliar 'dominant' dogs, their tail, as expected, wagged with a left-side bias. There are several variables that may have impacted the results of this study, including the stressful confinement of each dog, plus the unpredictable and uncontrollable environment, but it does tell us something important. It tells us that dogs have strong emotions and that exposure to positively associated stimuli elicits a different response to fear-inducing stimuli.

The tail is a communicative extension to a dog's body, but it also provides an essential tool for hunting. A rudder of sorts, it provides essential balance and support for changing direction at great speeds. Watch your dog running and you will see how the tail works as a sort of fifth leg.

Dogs without tails are unable to express a range of emotions to us and other dogs. It is important that owners become attuned to these dogs' feelings because they are expressed more subtly and often get missed. The more we miss our dogs' emotions, the more behavioural problems we get.

Nose

Smelling a red rose or the perfumed aroma of a passer-by can take our breath away. We are a species highly sensitive to olfactory signals and just one scent paired with an experience can create a sensory memory that lasts a lifetime. But when it comes to scent acuity, the human race has fallen far, far behind other species.

A black bear has been observed to smell and locate their prey from up to thirty kilometres away. A polar bear can detect the smell of a seal from a meter below thickened ice. Dogs can be trained to detect bombs and drugs, and research indicates they can even smell diabetes and some forms of cancer. In fact, their olfactory system is at least forty times better than the one behind our lousy nostrils.

The dog's nose is wet – a primitive survival adaptation for animals that rely on a keen sense of smell. A moist nose allows scents to absorb more effectively and inform the brain of what is out there, especially in the dark.

I believe that if a dog is highly motivated they can be suitable for scent work no matter what breed (with the exception of the beloved pug and bull dog), however the most common scent breeds are beagles, spaniels, shepherds, collies, pointers, bull terriers and hounds, such as the bassett, coon and blood hound.

Eyes

I do think that dogs and people see the world through a different lens and science backs up this belief. While we see a vast array of colours and shades, the dog's view of the world is much duller. As dichromats, dogs only have two types of colour-detecting cone cells, compared to the three that we have. This means that they see the world in yellows, blues and greys. Understanding a dog's vision helps us to realise that, quite literally, they can never see this world like we do. So why has their vision evolved so differently?

Dogs are crepuscular hunters, meaning that they hunt at dawn and dusk when their prey is most vulnerable. The canine's vision is focused on light and movement rather than colour perception.

Sometimes, Chester and Alma will see me from a distance and bark. They don't recognise me even though I can see exactly who they are and it takes several fast-paced steps before they too can recognise my familiar outlines.

WOLVES AND DOGS

Many experiments have been conducted comparing dog and wolf behaviour, particularly in relation to their social hierarchies. Scientists from a university in Budapest, Hungary, observed the development and behaviour of several domestic dogs and wolves that were hand raised by humans from birth.

Both the wolves and dogs were raised as pets, sharing food, beds and time with their human foster carers and other animals during their formative months. Scientists wanted to know if wolves would end up just like domestic dogs if they were raised the same way. A plate of food was offered to each dog and wolf, but was only provided if they made eye contact with the human.

While both attempted to access the food on their own, within two minutes, the domestic dogs began to look to the person. More interestingly, as the time went by, the difference between dogs and wolves increased, with the wolves not only unable to make eye contact with the human but also failing to learn that receiving the food was contingent on this behaviour.

This shines some light on the undeniable bond we share with dogs and how over tens of thousands of years we have grown to depend on one another for survival.

CHESTER AND PEOPLE

Chester and I regularly visit facilities including hospitals and elderly rest homes. But one of the many experiences that comes to mind is our first visit to an adult disability centre in Melbourne. Everyone knew we were coming, so I felt a combination of anxiety and excitement as we approached the building. None of the patients were able to express their emotions through speech, so I imagined it would be difficult to know if they were happy to see Chester, if they would like him or if they even wanted us there.

I remember that as we approached the entryway, most of the people inside had their heads down, eyes closed, or were gazing at the wall closest to them. I felt overcome with sadness as I watched these people unable to experience life the way I could. How ignorant I was.

While I was nervous, unsure of what their response would be, Chester seemed to be even more calm than usual. Alongside me, he casually strolled into the room and at that moment I saw the faces of these people transform. Their eyes lit up, their voices squealed in delight and they smiled. Even if they couldn't smile with their face, I could see it in their eyes. I could see it in their clapping hands, their movements towards us and, at that moment, I was filled with pride and gratitude. Chester got a lot of treats that day. When he licked their hands they laughed and the connection they made with this animal was extraordinary. I don't think any person on earth would have received the same response Chester did.

Even though there can be language barriers and cognitive and physical differences between people, we are all still the same. We all yearn for moments of purpose and happiness, and dogs can universally elicit these emotions within us.

MENTAL AND PHYSICAL EXERCISE

Exercise is a state of mind. It is about motivation, goals, self-improvement and overall health. There is no gadget or treadmill alone that makes us fit and healthy. These are tools to help get you there, but they are useless to your body if your mind isn't on board.

According to the Australian Institute of Health and Welfare, almost two thirds of us are overweight or obese. Since 1995, obesity has increased by 10 per cent and now one in four children is considered obese. It is a major risk factor for cardiovascular disease, Type 2 diabetes, some musculo-skeletal conditions and some cancers. In fact, obesity is the second highest contributor to poor health and even death, behind dietary risks.

Our mind plays a key role in weight gain. Depression can increase our intake of food, and decrease our physical activity levels. But, interestingly, exposure to sunlight can help us. If we can find moments of gratitude – as we explored in Chapter 12 – and bask in life's literal and proverbial sunshine, we can have a healthier mind and body. Over time, chronic depression can affect not just your emotions, but the brain's structure itself. MRI scans show that long-term depression results in a reduction of the frontal lobe and hippocampus. This suggests that our state of mind shapes not only how we feel, but also how we behave and potentially even how long we live.

While any physical or mental conditions are, of course, best assessed by a doctor or mental health expert, there are many different activities you can do with your dog to get your body moving and your mind active to help you live a happier, healthier life.

YOGA

An ancient mental, physical and spiritual practice dating back more than 2000 years, yoga only entered the Western zeitgeist fairly recently. What I love about it is that anyone and everyone can do it, for it is a practice that unites and controls the mind and body at the pace of the individual. For me, it is an essential ritual of my day. It is where I am able to spend time inside myself, dovetailing my thoughts and movements and building on all the teachings of dognitive therapy. It is a combined practice of mindfulness, acceptance and commitment therapy, cognitive behaviour therapy, motivation, cognitive empathy, calmness, cooperation and control. It is also about *consistency*, *patience* and *respect*. It is a complete workout of the mind, body and spirit.

It is also a workout that can be improved by the presence of your dog. Chester and Alma always practice with me each and every day and you too can try this with your dog.

Here is an outline of my daily yoga routine with my dogs, which you can adapt for you and your dog:

Firstly, we sit. Sometimes, the dogs both sit on my lap, so I encourage them to find their own space on the floor

I am completely *calm*, *cooperative* and *controlled* in my mind and immediately this is transferred to the dogs

I think about the day ahead and acknowledge the inevitable roadblocks I will encounter. I breathe heavily and deeply and with each exhalation I push out any negativity

When I am ready, I begin the practice of yoga with a long and tall stretch into the sky. I feel the muscles in my arms, legs and hands expand and contract as I push myself higher, and I enliven as the blood rushes through my body

With each movement, I hold it, breathe slowly and maintain my pose

When I fall, which I do, I get back up and try again. Embrace the failure and learn from it.

There are many simple yoga poses you can begin with, and each of them is an opportunity for you to strengthen your physical core as well as your mental prowess. You are strong, infallible and powerful in these moments and you begin the day believing that you are going to be the best you can be. To me, this is an essential ritual for your day with your dogs. You will engage in motions and pauses through yoga that push your limits and there will be times when your dog's excitement results in a licked face during the downward dog. It may not be ideal, but it's ok and if it happens, allow it.

Embrace the challenges of your mind and body and unleash your inner greatness. You are better than you think. You are far better than you ever give yourself credit for. Believe in yourself. Your dog needs you to.

Here are some basic yoga poses to start with. (The poses with an asterisk next to them will most likely result in you getting a licked face.)

Downward dog*

Warrior

Tree pose

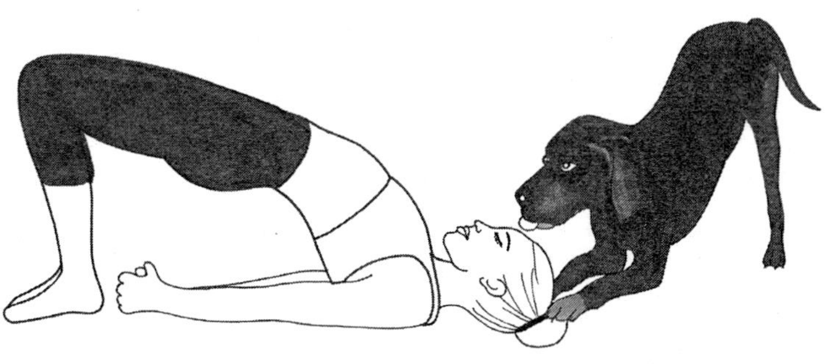

Bridge pose*

Triangle pose

Seated twist

Cobra pose*

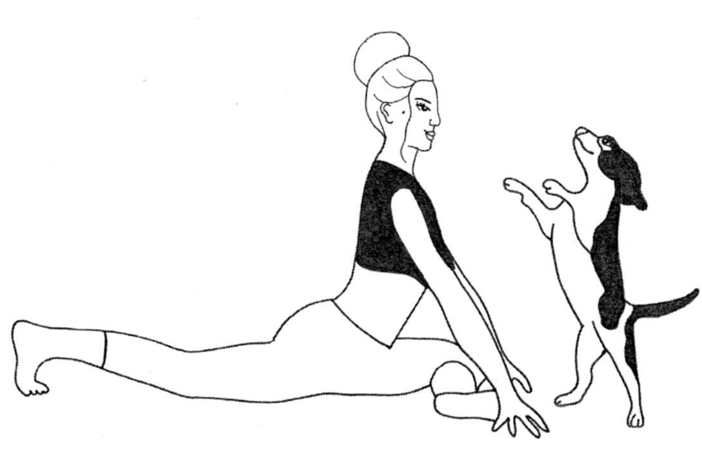

Pigeon pose

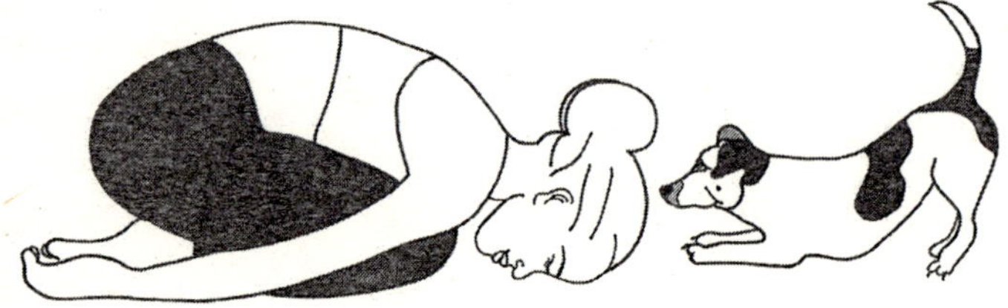

Child's pose*

Take fifteen minutes out of your day now and try it. How did you go?

Moving your body moves your mind. Research tells us that exercise makes us happier. But it is a sort of chicken or egg concept, isn't it? We need to feel good first to want to exercise. If we feel low, exercise seems to be the last thing on our minds. But for me, exercise is about ritual, not about how you are feeling at the time. It is about self-discipline and to do it consistently it needs to be a part of your life as much as food, water and sleep. For it to work, it needs to be separated from our emotions.

Exercise actually improves your mood. It increases the production of serotonin and endorphins, which, as we looked at in the previous chapter, are neurotransmitters that play a large part in our mood. Additionally, there is evidence that exercise improves your attention and memory too. Via a process called hippocampal neurogenesis, cells in the midbrain (specifically in the hippocampus) are produced and optimised by physical activity, resulting in an improved ability to focus, problem solve and retain information we absorb.

Could exercise be making us smarter? I do think scientists are on to something here. If exercise were a compulsory activity in everyday work and home life, I believe we would all have much better brains. The same goes for dogs.

BRAIN EXERCISE FOR YOUR DOG

The more we utilise the organ between our ears, the longer it lasts. The term neuroplasticity describes the ability of our brain to change throughout our lives. When we are confronted with a range of stimuli and experiences, our brain responds and reorganises itself. This means that the more we challenge our brain the more adaptable it is.

When I think of neuroplasticity, I think of dogs. If we collected hundreds of dogs from different environments, those who had mental stimulation, purpose and enrichment would undoubtedly have a very different brain to those who did not. Find out what your dog is interested in, what they are motivated by and create opportunities that are mentally purposeful. I cannot stress how important brain exercise is for you and your dog. An idle brain is a major determinant for mental health and wellbeing.

Here are my top five mind games for your dog:

1. Put away your dog's bowl and scatter food around your yard for your dog to find. Scattering or hiding food elicits natural exploratory behaviours in dogs, allowing them to use all their senses.

2. Teach your dog to associate a scent with a game and a treat. For example, package up some lavender and put it in front of your dog. When they go and smell it, reward them with a game of tug of war and treat. When your dog starts to make the association, hide the lavender and cue them to 'search' for it. When they find it, reward them with a game of tug of war. Make it really easy to start with, empowering and motivating them to engage. Eventually, you can teach them to discriminate this scent by placing it in a box, beside other similar boxes, and cue them to search for it. They will indicate by looking at you when they find the lavender box, resulting in meaningful play with their cooperative best friend (you).
3. Play a simple game of fetch, which can work so well to keep dogs mentally active. Reward them for returning the ball with a treat and throw it again straight away for them.
4. Play hide-and-seek in the backyard or park. This is so much fun and a great training tool for recall (the ability to come when called). You will need two people – one person with your dog and the other one hiding. When the person has hidden from sight, cue your dog to 'search' and allow them to go hunting.
5. Engage in a mental memory game where you hide a treat under a cup. When your dog nuzzles the cup or puts their paw on it, lift the cup and give them the treat. Some dogs are really good at this and you can introduce a second, third, forth or even fifth cup into the game.

Being 96 per cent genetically identical to a dog, there is a lot we have in common with them, especially when it comes to social bonding. Play is without a doubt one of the most important tools for enhancing a bond with your dog, just as it is with your children, friends and partner.

By interacting with others, we learn essential motor skills, understand how to cooperate and experience joy and laughter. This, ultimately, is when our brains are most stimulated and optimistic. As I often say, 'A play a day keeps the dog behaviourist away.' When we engage in cooperative fun, we become drawn to the activity and the person we are experiencing it with. It creates a bond of mutual trust and respect, the essential ingredients for a healthy and happy relationship.

SUMMARY

Your mind and body are two machines working together to optimise your survival and wellbeing. Just like us, dogs require care that protects and enhances their physical and mental health. Whilst dogs may bear different adaptations to us, they share more with us than we may realise. Good food, exercise and purpose are crucial to wellbeing as well as relaxation and positive thoughts. When both you and your dog experience these, not only may you live a longer and healthier life together, you will live a happier one too.

Did you know . . . *dogs having wet noses is an ancient adaptation for animals with an acute sense of smell? The wet surface allows them to absorb scents more effectively, helping them determine what is around them. Even the most primitive ancestor of man had a wet nose for the same purpose. Are dogs and humans more alike than we thought?*

17.

Setting Up For Success

If I could turn back time and undo all the mistakes I have made as a dog behaviourist, I would in an instant. I have made countless errors of judgement along the path to learning how to train animals. No matter what research is conducted, what psychological discoveries are made or how knowledgeable we become, dog 'experts' like myself can still learn more. The journey of understanding our relationship with dogs is a continuous learning curve and, for me, one that I look forward to each and every day.

Correction collars, shock implements and prong tools were among the coercive aids thrust upon me during the initial learning stages of my career. There is a clear science to punishment. Physical punishment that is significant enough can prevent a behaviour from occurring again – unless the dog desensitises to the punishment or the motivation to defy it overrides the motivation to obey. While I am not arguing against the research and effectiveness of physical (positive) punishment, I have throughout this book questioned the impact it has on a relationship and the reflection it has on the one delivering it. Are we setting our dogs up for failure or are we setting them up for success?

Punishment is one of those dirty words, like dominance. It is overused and misunderstood. Humans punish friends, family, colleagues and our dogs all the time. We may ignore our overbearing mother when they nag us, we may say 'no' when our dog jumps up against our car, or we may give our partner the silent treatment when they hurt our feelings. Unless we want everything in life to stay the same, punishment is essential to our social and physical survival.

I have used all the tools that were given to me early in my career, and many of them worked. Would I use some of them ever again? No. Why? Because there is a much more effective way to get the behaviour you want from a dog. And if you can't get what you want, learn to compromise. Isn't that part of any healthy and successful relationship?

If I could time travel back ten or so years, I would do things very differently. The truth is that no matter what you think you know about dog, your dog knows more. There are mistakes you have made that you cannot change, but your dog forgives you. They want you to be your best and, faithfully, they will stick by your side as you become a better person.

Mistakes are, sadly, essential. We tend to learn best by making them, usually because the error is something we consciously never want to happen again. Mistakes have a huge impact on our lives, our learning and our future decisions.

CASE STUDY

A collie mix named Bailey had recently been adopted into a home on acreage with a fellow dog and a loving couple who adored him. He had a special bed by the fire, rolling meadows to play in and a future that looked brighter than he could have ever imagined. One would assume that he was going to live happily ever after.

Weeks went by and Bailey's owners noticed something about him that they hadn't encountered with any of their other dogs before. His prey drive was insatiable. Each time a horse and its rider would trot past, he would gallop and pace up and down the boundary fence, utterly absorbed by the horse as prey. The owners, Joan and Barry, were kind, and had not only rescued Bailey, but over the years had adopted numerous donkeys in need of a home too. One particular donkey named Charlie lived at their property when Bailey first arrived, and upon their first encounter, it was apparent that Bailey saw the donkey as chump more than a chum.

Before Bailey arrived, Charlie the donkey would often graze among the garden beds in the front paddock. The gate was frequently open and Charlie would migrate across the acreage each day in search of the greener grass. But knowing Bailey's prey drive, Joan and Barry knew they would always have to ensure that Charlie was never within Bailey's reach.

Whilst Joan and Barry made every effort to keep them separated, Charlie's ventures to the front yard after escaping his paddock became a venture of regret. The meeting with Bailey was one that no witness could forget. Bailey spotted Charlie from the lounge and proceeded to leap off the couch, through the door and on to Charlie's nose within seconds. With each bellow of the donkey, Bailey's teeth gripped deeper. Joan and Barry pulled and prodded Bailey from left to right attempting to distract him, but the prey drive was too high. They later described the experience to me as if it lasted for hours. But eventually, Barry pried Bailey's mouth open and Charlie bolted to the paddock. Charlie's nose gushed out a fountain of blood and, after Bailey was put back inside, he was tended to and patched back together with twenty stitches.

Bailey's electric collar was used to punish him severely after the attack. Within twenty metres of his target, Bailey would be quickly reminded that Charlie was off limits.

Joan and Barry called me the next day. I remember thinking to myself, 'This does not sound promising.' With respect to an insatiable prey drive in a dog, anyone who guarantees a shift in behaviour through training is promising something that isn't really completely in their control. Nevertheless, I made the visit, sat down by the fire in their lounge and met the family, of which Bailey was clearly a part.

They told me about Bailey and where he had come from. They had felt very sorry for him and after suddenly losing their beloved lab just months earlier, Bailey had big paws to fill. I put the lead on Bailey (two leads actually) and took him out to observe his behaviour in view of Charlie the donkey. Bailey was very timid around Charlie, avoidant even, aware that his behaviour from the previous week would be punished again.

We worked on some basic training, talked about barriers and prevention, but whilst I gave them an inch of hope, I knew I'd have to take away much more. It would be irresponsible for me to guarantee Bailey could change. How could I promise that to this family? I knew it was best to find Bailey a more suitable lifestyle, I was just mustering up the courage to break this to his owners.

As Barry led Charlie back to the paddock. Joan and I sat down to discuss the future and what they would do to keep Charlie safe. We made sure all the doors were closed and let Bailey off-lead to discuss the plan in more detail. It was strange because as we talked more and more, we noticed that Bailey was no longer beside us. It was upon this realisation that I will never forget Joan's response. Her face went white and the terror in her voice alerted me that Charlie was in grave trouble. I never knew there was a doggy door in the kitchen and upon releasing Bailey from my control, he had returned outside to Charlie. 'Bailey, NO!'

I ran through the kitchen door, pushing through the thick air as I struggled to catch Bailey. But as I approached him, it was too late. Bailey had begun rounding Charlie into the garden bed and only one would get out. Charlie bellowed in fear and, as I got closer, the attack that had been retold to me previously was being relived. In desperation, Joan and Barry tried to lead Charlie back to the paddock and I found myself completely without thought, in between dog and mule.

Fear subconsciously dominated my behaviour and I fought for that donkey, risking my own life. The three of us tumbled in silence through the garden beds, as Bailey's resolve became more and more hardened. I kicked, held and pulled, and the adrenaline in me left me completely numb. Eventually, I stupidly put my hands into Bailey's mouth, which was attached to Charlie's face, and, with his legs in one arm, my other hand pushed down and into his mouth in the hope of prying it open. I could feel his teeth piercing my hand, but there was no pain. All I could think of was that the more my hand was there, the less Charlie's face was.

After what had seemed like an eternity, Bailey tired and let go. Charlie ran for safety, barely able to move from shock. As I watched him run off, Bailey and I lay on the ground in complete defeat. I mustered the energy to stand and picked him up, taking him into the run that had been built for him when he was home alone. Covered in blood from ear to toe, both of us sat in that run and all I could think of was that donkey's welfare and that I wasn't sure whose blood I was covered in.

The vet was called and I left after discovering most of the blood that masked me was my own. Charlie lost a lot of blood that night but survived, and to this day remains a part of Joan and Barry's life. Bailey didn't stay. It wasn't fair to Bailey or Charlie. The expectations on Bailey to change what was truly ingrained in his instincts were too high, as was the risk that it could always happen again. We would have set him up for failure each and every day, and a simple human error may have ended Charlie's life, not to mention Bailey's.

Bailey was soon adopted by a man in the suburbs who adores him. And whilst Joan and Barry's hearts were truly broken, it was a decision that was best for everyone, especially Bailey.

Some of you reading this may say he should be put to sleep, others may shake their heads with worry that if a dog can attack a donkey, why wouldn't they attack a child. But the truth is dogs have a lot to live up to. Whilst we may boast that our dogs are descendants of the wolf, we still want them to behave like lambs. Dogs with a high prey drive do not inherently see children as prey. At some point, we have got to start taking responsibility for our dog's behaviour. If a dog can't live up to our expectations, shouldn't we be finding a safe and common ground instead of discarding them as unusable rubbish?

The purpose of this book is to get you thinking. This was not an unresolved case, where the dog couldn't live in harmony with the donkey. This was a case in which we acknowledged that Bailey may be able to learn to avoid Charlie and that Joan and Barry may be able to ensure Charlie was always safe in his paddock, but at the same time even if the risk was reduced significantly, the consequence of a recurrence would be too dire. We learnt that it was best to set all up for success, instead of setting all up for failure.

When we are modifying a behaviour or changing the way people work with their animals, we are completely responsible for them and their welfare. While mistakes are essential to progress, they should never compromise the safety or wellbeing of anyone involved.

CHESTER AND I

These days I rarely find myself asking anything of Chester. I don't need to. After years of building a relationship based on trust and respect, we both agree that being *calm*, *cooperative* and *controlled* are the best ways to get what we want. We have an agreement, which works beautifully, but it wasn't always like this.

When I was at the infantile stages of my training career, I remember running my very first behaviour consultations for free as nobody would pay me. The more I researched, the less I felt like knew, and I began to second-guess myself not just as a trainer but also as a person. My personal life was turbulent and every aspect of my mind's instability was reflected in Chester's behaviour. From a confident and outgoing dog, he became reactive and nervous, easily startled by other dogs or loud noises. In what felt like overnight, I didn't recognise him. The truth was, he didn't recognise me either.

If I took Chester to the beach, he would run up to the dogs playing with a ball and antagonise them with lunging and pushy behaviours. 'Get your bloody dog away from here. You shouldn't be here with a dog like that!' people would say to me. I would run up and apologise while putting Chester back on-lead.

If you have a dog who you just don't understand, I get it! I have been there. I have sat next to Chester and asked myself if I can really help him. Am I a bad dog owner? Am I irresponsible? Is it true what they say about this breed? I asked every question I could think of to try to figure out why this dog I loved more than anything had all of a sudden become unrecognisable.

My anxiety persisted, lasting several months, to the point where I had not only become a recluse, but I had fallen into a spiralling hole of negativity. And the more negative I became, the worse Chester's behaviour was. I had been reinforcing Chester's anxious, needy behaviours through my own anxious and needy mental state. We have an enormous influence over those we love and while our energy and spirit is contagious, so too is our darkness. Just as we can easily influence and capture the good, we can just as easily influence and capture the bad and the ugly.

Who you are and how you feel trickles into the chemistry between you and your dog. I was living proof of this back then. I didn't have anyone to tell me that my dog was a reflection of me, but eventually Chester did and I was ready to listen.

Despite my setbacks, I am also an example of why you should feel hopeful. Now, years later, I look at Chester cuddled up like a kidney bean at my feet and reminisce on the journey we have taken to get here. It occurs to me that this journey isn't over. We continue to learn and experience this world together, each day discovering something new.

You have so much influence over your dog as their guardian. This world is stressful to them. It is filled with ebbs and flows of uncontrollable uncertainty. Confidence and self-assurance exists only if you allow it, and only if you empower it through capturing the good. Confidence and self-assurance provided by a leader pollinate a unique and fulfilling relationship between man and dog, which blossoms into a friendship so great it becomes a part of your soul.

SETTING YOURSELF UP FOR FAILURE

For you and me, failure is an inevitable part of life. But the difference between failing and being set up for failure is huge. Being set up for failure occurs when the goal is unachievable. It is a form of bullying when the person setting the goal knows that the participant will never reach it. Sometimes the bully is external, but sometimes the bully comes from within.

Sadly, dog owners set their dogs up to fail every day. When we ask a dog to do something and they don't do it, we punish them, rarely stopping to ask ourselves why the dog wouldn't obey in the first place. Did they understand you? Were you consistent last time? Is the task too hard? Are they feeling anxious? Did you reinforce their anxieties last time this happened? Do you actually mean what you say? Are you going to follow through? Are they sick? Can they get away from the threat? Do they trust you? The list continues.

Whenever our dog does not behave as we ask, it is almost invariably because we have set an unachievable goal and because we have not used CPR: a *calm*, *patient* and *respectful* approach.

Have we stopped to think about the dog's point of view? If we do, it is usually from an anthropomorphic and human-centric outlook. For instance, if our dog is not happily interacting with a child that has approached them, we may think, *But he loves kids!* I love kids too, but if they start to corner me and poke me in the face, I would soon let them know how I felt. But dogs can't always understand our intentions and motivations and they can't express their feelings as fluently as they can to their fellow species. They depend on us as their guardians and their guides, and although they may share a similar level of cognition to a very young child, they don't deserve to be treated as a substitute.

Interestingly, when a dog is treated strictly with a 'Do as I say' approach, we see similar behavioural issues arise in them as we do for those who are mollycoddled by their owners. Research on human parenting backs this up too, with studies showing that children who are parented with the stern 'suck it up' approach are just as likely to develop unhealthy attachments and anxieties as those who receive cotton-wool parenting. Both styles are liable to instil fear and frustration in dependents. A happy medium to parenting and dog ownership is recommended, where a nurturing, understanding and supportive guardian oversees the health and wellbeing of those they protect.

This got me to thinking about dogs that are punished when displaying hyperreactive behaviours, such as growling, snapping and lunging towards an anxiety-provoking stimulus. When a dog growls, they are communicating. It is one of the first few warnings they diplomatically give to a person or animal before the situation escalates. By correcting this behaviour with a harsh punishment, what are we telling our dog? This punishment does not change how they feel about whoever is approaching them, it just teaches them that the next time this happens, they shouldn't growl. However, this may actually encourage them to snap or lunge instead.

This is where some people will say to me, 'But he just snaps without warning.' No, he doesn't. He has given countless subtle cues leading up to that moment, possibly over weeks or months. He has attempted to communicate his feelings, sometimes even being punished for it. So now he just does what he has been taught and bites.

If you think you may be setting your dog up for failure, stop! Your dog will never grow up to look after herself. That is your job. So for him to trust and respect you, as well as behave in a socially positive manner, you must set him up for success.

SETTING YOURSELF UP FOR SUCCESS

Success is about knowing what you can and can't control, and choosing the path that will lead you to a positive outcome. The mark of a great leader is one who identifies the strengths and weaknesses of their followers and sets up challenges that empower and build confidence within them. They seize the good moments and encourage others to 'have a go', unafraid of failure because the attempt is the indicator of success, not the outcome.

As eternal dependents, dogs need safe instructions from us. With anxiety being such a frequent cause of destructive and dangerous behaviours in dogs, there must be something we are doing wrong. Remember that anxiety is provoked by uncertainty, so if we are not able to provide a positive and predictable existence for our dog, we are not setting them up for success. So how do we do this?

Eight ways to success for you and your dog

1. Know what you want.
2. Set achievable goals for you and your dog and take your time reaching them. Remember it is the attempt not the outcome that is important, so it is vital that the attempt is a positive experience.

3. Link CPR through every interaction you have with those in your life. If you want your dog to trust you, you must give CPR.
4. Apply cognitive empathy (i.e. distanced, rational compassion) and think from your dog's point of view. Don't get frustrated or angry: that is a reflection of your failings, not theirs. If they don't do what you want, ask yourself why instead of why not.
5. If you cannot control an environment, don't enter it with your dog.
6. Don't be afraid to fail, but be willing to learn from failure, remembering there is a big difference between failure and being set up for it.
7. Always encourage the 3 Cs for both you and your dog. If you find that neither of you is *calm*, *cooperative* or *controlled*, you have pushed yourself too far. Take a step back and re-enter the path to success, no matter how narrow and long it may be.
8. Celebrate the highs, no matter how small the gains may be.

Being set up for success is not really about success itself, it is about developing a positive attitude and self-esteem.

Amy Cuddy, a social psychologist from America, delivered a talk a few years ago about how your body language shapes who you are. She talked about how the way we sit and the way we stand tells others and ourselves about who we are. According to Cuddy, our thoughts and feelings can be determined by our posture, and if we adopt a confident physical position, we can convince others as well as ourselves that we are successful.

Research attests to this. One study looked at the differences between people who were asked to adopt either assertive or insecure poses. The hypothesis being that participants who displayed more overt and confident postures would not only be perceived to be more successful, but their own brains would believe it as well. Among other hormones, the key stress hormone, cortisol, was tested before and after the postures were adopted. Researchers found that those who adopted the assertive poses had lower cortisol levels than those who displayed more negative postures, telling us that their body was under less stress, and was less reactive and more confident. When I think about this study, I think about the 3 Cs. When we adopt a *calm*, *cooperative* and *controlled* disposition, we are more successful.

In addition to the cortisol comparisons, researchers also examined whether postures could actually affect the outcome of certain stressful events. One event that came to mind was a job interview, and in an attempt to control all variables, the dependent variable was whether or not performing these assertive postures in privacy for two minutes prior to the interview would affect the result. A selection team, blinded to the fact that they were participating in a psychological study, were asked to review the video recordings of all participants. They found that those who adopted the confident poses were invariably favoured for the jobs.

Amy Cuddy made an interesting remark in her lecture that 'bodies can change our mind, our mind can change behaviours and behaviours can change outcomes'.

You can effectively 'fake it till you believe it', according to Cuddy and her colleagues. We have to believe in ourselves, even if it starts with standing up straight, opening our arms wide and breathing in positive energy. We are the only ones who can control our journey and our destiny and we owe it to ourselves to believe we can achieve anything.

Dogs don't follow insecure, indecisive, inconsistent people because they want to. They do so because they have to. If you observe wild wolves, you see confident and assertive postures in the leaders. They are calm, cooperative and controlled. They are consistent, patient and respectful of members in their group and they believe in themselves. Consequently, their pack believes in them too and together they form a cohesive family that is successful and survives.

You create the success in your life. You also create the success or demise of your dog. Stand up tall and believe you are a success. It is completely determined by you. It does not involve money or materials. Success is not reflected by the size of your house or your car, how you look or where you sit on the corporate hierarchy. Success is how you feel about yourself. It is about empathy, gratitude, acceptance and respect. It is about being able to look in the mirror and love who you are – a kind person who does their best every day.

Nothing of material value has value to your soul or your happiness. In science, religion and philosophy, nobody has ever proven that acquiring material things leads to success. Rather, success is within us already and whether we experience it or suppress it depends on our self-perception. Your dog will let you know how successful you are. Their relationship with you, others and themselves is a reflection of who they think you are. And that's what is so equally petrifying and elating about it. Dogs remind us every day that we are better than we think, that we are still yet to reach our full potential and that we can always be better to those around us.

Success to me is a journey that I believe I will travel along for the rest of my life. I don't ever want there to be a final destination. My desire for success will continue until the day I die and I won't know how far I have come until the dog laying by my side tells me. They will always, faithfully, tell you the truth.

My dogs don't care about my finances or my career. They are more interested in the strength of my character: how good I am as a person, my leadership skills, my kindness and my understanding of others. And these are the traits most difficult to obtain and sustain in life. My dogs inspire me each and every day to be better, to be happier and to feel more grateful. They remind me that life is precious and never guaranteed. They are my light, my love and my life.

You see, dogs are already successful. They embody all the qualities that we spend a lifetime trying to acquire. They are our teachers and our motivators; they are the best part of us. Dogs are the most successful people I know. Let them lead the way along a journey to success.

Conclusion

As your dog faithfully follows, sits patiently and looks to you for guidance, realise how important your role in their world is. We have brought these dogs into our lives for various purposes, never once asking the dog if it was okay. And as we go on to teach our dogs the most extraordinary tricks and skills, for our benefit, our dogs have been the ones with the superior traits all along. Dogs bear the qualities that we as humans spend a lifetime trying to acquire. Their inherent loyalty is admirable. Their ability to be mindful and grateful gives them authority as our spiritual leaders. Their need to exist in a relationship based on mutual trust and respect inspires us to be better, earning those virtues through empathy and kindness.

We know more than ever before about our faithful counterparts, with science divulging extraordinary secrets of the canine mind. And as we learn more about them, we realise that who they are is not that different to us. That the thousands of years we have spent moulding their minds and bodies to our liking has ultimately moulded them into a reflection of us.

They can inspire greatness in us, but also bring out our darkness, as we show our true character to them. Our consistency, patience and respect are challenged as we get to know how our dogs think and whether we can coexist successfully. But the success of this relationship invariably relies on the human. Dogs are already better people than we are. And whilst we may have the proverbial upper hand, it is time we realise that they are our equals. Any living being brought into your home and family deserves respect. Whilst we may be their eternal providers, that has never been through a choice of their own.

Take the time to get to know who your dog really is. Discover their likes, dislikes, hobbies and fears. Find out what makes them anxious, what their favourite food is and when they are most happy. Ask them questions, don't tell them facts. Listen to them, don't talk at them. Open your mind to understanding their behaviours and respect the role you play in the relationship. This is what a good friend does. And as we continue to boast that dog is man's best friend – a proclamation held high and proud – it's time we start to reciprocate.

Summary

The table below summarises the key learnings of this book. In each chapter, we have looked at what the most helpful traits and virtues are to underpin our thoughts, choices, emotions and behaviours. The table shows the types of behaviours and mindsets you should strive for, and how these will improve not only your own life, but that of your dog.

TRAITS AND VIRTUES	YOU	YOUR DOG
Consistent Patient Respectful	Become someone who is true to your word, who has empathy and who is understanding. These traits help to define leadership and those around you will want to follow.	Your dog will start to see you as a leader. They will follow your guidance because they want to, not because they feel they have to.

Calm Cooperative Controlled	Find ways to exist as a calm, cooperative and controlled person no matter what stress you are under. Apply some acceptance and commitment therapy (ACT) techniques and sit with any distress you may feel. Realise what rational choices you have and make them without using emotions.	You provide leadership by rewarding positive mindsets and behaviours. Your dog will start to feel more content, more in control and more optimistic about themselves and their relationship with you.
Trust	Trust your own judgement. Consider your options and make decisions based on what you believe in.	Show your dog they can trust you by setting them up for success in times of uncertainty. If you think your dog will fail in a situation, remove them from it immediately and give them something positive to focus on. Don't risk the breakdown of trust. It is difficult to regain.
Empathy	Always consider the points of view of others, however, do not adopt the emotional chaos that can result from over-empathising.	Thinking from your dog's point of view makes them feel understood and respected.

Predictability Controllability	Try to predict and control environments where you can but at the same time acknowledge that you can't always. In those times, you adopt the 3 Cs and find a way to remove yourself from the situation if needed.	Your dog stops continuously trying to predict and control their environment because they trust you will do it successfully for them.
Mindfulness	Sit, breathe and be. Focus on the present and accept what you are facing.	Your dog is already mindful. Watch them whenever you feel overwhelmed. Let them think you are mindful too.
Seizing good moments	Look for the great moments in your day, including the ones your dog provides.	Your dog will start to offer good behaviours all the time, knowing that you will consistently, patiently and respectfully look for the good in them.
Motivation	Remind yourself that every goal you have is achievable. Celebrate the tiny stuff, it's what is most important. When you fail, which you will, embrace it, learn from it and see it as being a step closer to success.	Your dog will benefit from your active lifestyle. They will also benefit from the energy you invest in your relationship with them.

Loyalty	Choose those you love and trust, and stick by them.	Your dog has the leadership role here. Appreciate their faithfulness. Learn from them.
Gratitude	You are alive. Life is a miracle. Find simple things to be grateful for each day. The more you look, the more you will find.	Your dog is instinctively grateful. They will benefit from your own personal gratitude as you demonstrate being a more calm, cooperative and controlled leader.
Wellbeing and your body	Take care of every inch of your body. Nobody else will.	You dog's behaviour and mental state are ultimately controlled by you. Take care of them. Listen to them and respect them. Nobody else will.
Rewards and punishments	Work hard and reward yourself when you complete each step towards a larger goal. Know what you want and go after it.	Know what your dog likes and dislikes. Reward them with what they want each time they display the 3 Cs. But be prepared: the more you reward, the more your dog will offer you good behaviours. You may need lots of rewards handy.

Acknowledgements

Firstly, I want to thank you, the reader. You have picked up this book with an open mind and a willingness to think about yourself and your dogs a little differently. Thank you for looking at your dog and accepting that perhaps part of their behaviour is reflected in yours. If you don't accept this yet, don't worry. There was I time when I didn't either. But you will. And when you do, it will blow your mind.

To the team at Penguin. Wow, what a team! Ben Ball, Sarah Fairhall, Sam Sainsbury, Sam Mills, Adrian Potts, Johannes Jakob, Kimberley Atkins, Jackie Money, the extraordinary sales team, Alex Cearns, Louisa Maggio, and every member of the team that has welcomed my visits with wide smiles and doggy pats. You have believed in me and my passion that sits well and truly outside the square of traditional dog training. Thank you for your patience, support and open-mindedness.

My beautiful friends. Only a handful are not dogs, so you must be special! Sie Wey, Steve, Melissa, Becks, Ange,

Mark and Giu. To my sisters, Em, Tab, and Angie: three magnificent women who I adore completely.

Mum, you are a woman of great strength and character. You are the woman who never gives up and fights for what you believe in. I have never known anyone like you and am eternally grateful for having picked up those apples from the tree.

Thank you to my ever-loving and supportive better half Chris. I hope that each day I make you proud, just as you inspire awe in me each and every day. You have always believed in me. You have known that my heart and soul lives for creating a better life for dogs and you have encouraged me to write a book that is fearless and true to what I believe in. I could have never done this without your support. I adore you completely and couldn't imagine any lifetime without you by my side.

Alma, you are an example of how the most vulnerable can be equally strong and wise. A lifetime of hardship challenged by resilience and strength makes you a better person than I could ever be. You are a phenomenal woman, though a dog. I am in awe of your patience and trust. Your fumbling feet at my side, willing to follow me wherever I go without question, make you one of the best friends I have ever had. I will never let you down.

Chester. There is this overwhelming love I have for you that cannot be done justice with mere words. You are the embodiment of everything good in this world. If I could be half the person you are, I would be twice the person I strive for. You remind me to focus on the good and make the most of every moment, for I never know when you may no longer be at my side. You are a glorious burden, because every moment we share is one less moment to spend together.

I know you won't live forever, but I know that together, we have a chance to show the world that man and dog are a force that can achieve a kinder and better world. Thank you for being my light, my life and my love. You, Chester are my soulmate.

Lastly, to the dogs. You are the best people. I hope your human agrees.